A Taste of Georgia

ANOTHER SERVING

Published by
Newnan Junior Service League
Newnan, Georgia

The purpose of the Newnan Junior Service League is to foster interest in social, educational, cultural, health and civic conditions of our community and to support civic and charitable enterprises by efficient volunteer service of its members.

This book was published and copyrighted in 1991 under the name:
A Taste of Georgia II, In The Southern Manner

Proceeds from the sale of *A Taste of Georgia, Another Serving* will be returned to the community through projects sponsored by the Newnan Junior Service League.

In 1985, the Newnan Junior Service League decided to begin compiling a new cookbook to be used as a companion to our still very successful first book, *A Taste of Georgia*. The recipes found in *A Taste of Georgia, Another Serving* have been tested in the same high standard as our previously published cookbook.
The magnolia denotes tried and true traditional Southern recipes.

For the past eight years many people have donated their time and talents to make this book a reality. The League is truly indebted to all who helped in the creation of this book.

Cookbook Committee Chairman: Penny Williams
Art: Anne Jarrell Berry
Proofreading: Cathy Powell
Recipe Collection: Eileen Muzio
Tasting: Debbie Lanier, Sammy Reeves
Testing: Cathy Powell
Typing: Deborah Bennett, Cindy Yeager
President, 1991-1992: Linda Mitchell
Cookbook Chairman, 1990-1992: Carol Markham

Cover Photograhpy: Jim Hynds
HyndSight Photography
Carrolton, Georgia

Props: Retta's Antiques
College Park, Georgia
Tivoli Restaurant
Newnan, Georgia

Cover Design: Julie Genda McKinney
Genda Designs
Newnan, Georgia

The Newnan Junior Service League is proud to offer *A Taste of Georgia, Another Serving.* We hope you will enjoy it!

NEWNAN JUNIOR SERVICE LEAGUE
ACTIVE MEMBERS 1990-91

Mrs. David Asher (Tammy)
Mrs. Michael Barber (Julia)
Mrs. Gregory Bekius (Nancy)
Mrs. William Berry, III (Anne)
Mrs. Duke Blackburn (Lynn)
Mrs. Tommy Brevelle (Suzy)
Mrs. Joseph Brown (Sally)
Mrs. Tim Carroll (Beth)
Mrs. Roddy Clifton (Connie)
Mrs. David Cotton (Pat)
Mrs. John Herbert Cranford (Carolyn)
Mrs. Frank Eldridge (Edie)
Mrs. Dave Fargason (Donna)
Mrs. Frank Farmer (Melody)
Mrs. John Fielding (Kandi)
Mrs. David Franks (Carol)
Mrs. Mitch Ginn (Mary Jane)
Mrs. Peter Gosh (Lisa)
Mrs. Jay Haire (Tina)
Mrs. Leo Harland (Jan)
Mrs. Bill Hartselle (Joan)
Mrs. Rocky Hawkins (Sally)
Mrs. Hugh Heflin, Jr. (Julia)
Mrs. David LaGuardia (Jane)

Mrs. Walter Lonergan (Ginny)
Mrs. Terry Lunsford (Frances)
Mrs. Dennis McEntire (Sally)
Mrs. William McGuire (Ginny)
Mrs. Frank Marchman (Beth)
Mrs. Scott Markham (Carol)
Mrs. Robert Merrell (Sam)
Mrs. Stephen Mitchell (Linda)
Mrs. Thomas Morningstar (Donna)
Mrs. Hutch Murphy (Mary Jane)
Mrs. Andrew Muzio (Eileen)
Mrs. Joe Powell (Cathy)
Mrs. Joel Richardson (Ingrid)
Mrs. Bob Sandlin (Pam)
Mrs. Mitch Sherwood (Cindy)
Mrs. Charles V. Slomka (Tricia)
Mrs. Steve Southard (Jennifer)
Mrs. Stephen Sprayberry (Colleen)
Mrs. Larry Strickland (Montie)
Mrs. Kyle Tatum (Kathy)
Mrs. John Tucker (Carol)
Mrs. Lisa Van Houten
Mrs. Donald Walls (Leigh)
Mrs. W.E. Yeager (Cindy)

WE ARE GRATEFUL TO EACH CONTRIBUTOR
WHO DONATED RECIPES FOR USE IN

A Taste of Georgia
Another Serving

UNFORTUNATELY, LACK OF SPACE
PREVENTED US FROM INCORPORATING
ALL THESE PRIZED RECIPES

PEARS POACHED IN REDWINE WITH CRÈME BRULÉE SAUCE

PEARS

8	ripe Bartlett or other pears	2	c. honey
4	c. red wine	1	cinnamon stick

Bring red wine and honey to a boil. Core the pears and with a knife, carve off portions of peeling to create a design (swirls, stripes, etc. use your imagination). Set pears upright into the red wine syrup and let simmer on low fo 5 - 10 minutes, depending on ripeness of pears. Allow to cool in the syrup.

*This recipe can be made with a white wine and your choice of herbs and spices, such as mixed peppercorns, bay leaves, rosemary and thyme.

SAUCE CRÈME BRULÉE

7	egg yolks	2	T. vanilla extract
1/4	c. sugar	2	T. Grand Marnier
2	c. heavy cream		

In a mixing bowl, whisk together the yolks and sugar for about 2 minutes. Set aside. In a double boiler, over medium heat, bring the creme and vanilla to a boil. Add the cream mixture to the egg mixture and whisk quickly, so the eggs won't curdle. Cook until smooth. Add the Grand Marnier and allow to cool before serving. Pour this sauce onto the serving plate before placing pear in center.

Chef Leif Petersen
Tivoli Restaurant
Newnan, Georgia

*To make heart design in sauce, as shown on front cover photo, place drops of raspberry puree where heart is desired. With a toothpick, placed in front of the drop, drag back through the drop. Viola! A Heart!

Recipes that make Special Gifts

Spiced Cocoa Mix
Elm Street School Cheese Wafers
Cheese Pennies
Spiced Pecans
Seasoned Oyster Crackers
Flavored Vinegar
Pomander Balls
Artichoke Relish
Pepper Sherry Sauce
Jezebel Sauce
Bean Soup Mix
Homemade Cordials
Soap Crayons
Silly Putty
Homemade Chocolate Sauce

Recipes for the·Grill
See Index

African Sauce for Grilled Steak
Elm Street School BBQ Sauce
Turkish Yogurt Marinade
Italian Wine Marinade
BBQ Sauce
Chicken Marinade
Mexican Grilled Chicken

Microwave Recipes
See Index

Microwave Mushroom Topping
Microwave White Sauce
Microwave Hollandaise Sauce
Microwave Chocolate Sauce
French Onion Soup
Microwave Macaroni & Cheese
Microwave Candy

Recipes from Area Restaruants

Dailey's Blood Mary
Carlos McGee's Bloody Mary
Hogan's Heros' Bacon and Bleu
Cheese Soup
Hogan's Heros' Roasted Red Peppers
Buckhead Diner Peach Bread Pudding
City Café House Dressing
In Clover Sundae
In Clover Lace Cookies
City Café Chocolate Mousse Cake
Tivoli's Poached Pears

Low Fat Recipes
See Index

Low Sodium Seasoning I and II
Miracle Soup
Oat Bran Muffins
Tan Rice
Bulgar Casserole
Mexican Grilled Chicken
Marinated Grilled Fish Steaks
Smoked Trout
Fish Teriyaki
Tropical Sherbet

Recipes that are Traditionally Southern

See magnolia symbol

CONTENTS

"LOVE IN A COTTAGE."—"Never Mind; Don't Cry, Pet, I'll Do all the Cooking."

By permission of Harper Bros., New York.

The Dixie Cook-Book (1888)

B E V E R A G E S

Tea Set

Demitasse cup and saucer fitted with café royale spoons:
fill with Brandy and a sugar cube and serve flambé.

BEVERAGES

SPICED COCOA MIX

2 cups nonfat dry milk
  powder
1/2 cup powdered nondairy
  creamer
1/4 cup unsweetened cocoa
  powder
1/3 cup sifted powdered sugar

3/4 teaspoon ground cinnamon
1/2 teaspoon ground nutmeg
Boiling water
Instant coffee crystals
  (optional)
Coffee liqueur (optional)
Stick cinnamon (optional)

Combine dry milk, creamer, cocoa powder, sugar, cinnamon and nutmeg. Mix thoroughly. For each serving combine 1/3 cup mix and 3/4 cup boiling water in a mug. Stir. Add coffee crystals, stick cinnamon, or liqueur to taste.

Mrs. Don Tomlinson (Jane)
Asheville, N.C.

ICED COFFEE A LA MODE

Yield: 6 servings

1 quart coffee ice cream
6 cups strong fresh coffee,
 chilled
1/2 cup whipping cream

1 teaspoon sugar
1/2 teaspoon almond extract
Mint leaves
Red cherries

Put 1 large scoop ice cream in tall glass. Fill with chilled coffee. Top with whipped cream that has been sweetened with sugar and flavored with almond extract. Garnish with mint leaves and a red cherry.

Mrs. Frank Marchman (Beth Candler)

HOT APPLE CIDER
Fragrance in house is wonderful

Yield: 1 quart

1 quart apple cider or apple
 juice
1 (4 inch) cinnamon stick
8 whole cloves

8 whole allspice
1/3 cup light brown sugar
Butter for garnish

Combine all ingredients except butter. Bring to a boil but do not let mixture bubble. Simmer 10 minutes. Strain into mugs and top with 1/2 teaspoon of butter.

Mrs. Bryant Hunter (Victoria)

Vanilla Coffee: Add 2 teaspoons vanilla to each cup of brewed coffee.

LIME SHERBET PUNCH

Yield: 100 servings

4 packages (4 ounce) lime
  jello; not sugar free
1 quart hot water
1 dozen lemons, juiced

1 large can pineapple juice;
  unsweetened
3 cartons (1/2 gallon) lime
  sherbet

Dissolve jello in hot water. Add lemon juice and pineapple juice. Add enough water to make 2 gallons. Chill. To each gallon of liquid, add 3/4 of 1 gallon of sherbet. Fold in and let melt a little. Serves about 100 people.

Mrs. Guilford Connally

TANGERINE PUNCH

Yield: 2 1/2 quarts

1/2 cup sugar
1 cup water
1 quart tangerine juice

1/4 cup fresh lime juice
1/2 cup grapefruit juice
1 quart ginger ale

Boil sugar and water 5 minutes. Cool and add juices. Combine with ginger ale when ready to serve.

NOTE: Minute Maid makes a good frozen tangerine juice.

Mrs. Frank Marchman (Beth Candler)

Luncheon Tea:
  Add pineapple juice along with lemon juice and sugar to taste. Garnish with fresh mint.

BEVERAGES

CHRISTMAS PUNCH

Yield: 40 (3-ounce) servings

1 quart cranberry juice
1 quart dry ginger ale
2 cups lemonade

1 cup orange juice
2 cups Southern Comfort

Combine ingredients and serve chilled or with ice.

Mrs. Walter M. Lonergan II (Ginny)

SYLLABUB
Traditional Southern Christmas drink

Yield: 12 to 16 servings

1 1/2 cups whole milk
1 quart whipping cream

2 cups sugar
1 to 1 1/2 cups cream sherry

Mix milk and cream together. Stir in sugar until well dissolved. Add sherry. Be sure milk is very cold and kept so, or your syllabub will be a failure. Churn with a syllabub churn or mix with egg beater. Knock down the first foam with the back of a large spoon, as it is too full of air. After this, as foam forms, dip off the top into tall glasses and keep churning. If any is left, keep well chilled in refrigerator and it will churn just as well later.

(This is a good treat for children, and they love to help with the churning.)

George Richard Ellis
Americus, Georgia

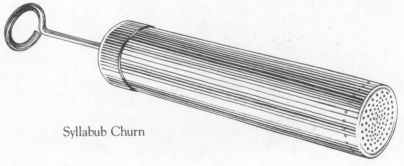

Syllabub Churn

ORANGE EGGNOG PUNCH
From "The Delta Family Cookbook"

Yield: 12 to 15 servings

2 quarts prepared eggnog
1 (6 ounce) can frozen orange
  juice, undiluted

1 (28 ounce) bottle ginger ale

Chill all ingredients. Mix together in medium-sized punch bowl.

Nadine Weekes
Orlando, Florida

MOCHA PUNCH

Yield: 3 1/2 Quarts

2 cups boiling water
1/2 cup instant coffee
  granules
1 1-oz. square unsweetened
  chocolate, melted
1/3 cup sugar

1/2 gallon vanilla ice cream,
  softened
1 quart milk
Sweetened whipped cream
Grated chocolate

Combine water and instant coffee granules, blending well. Stir in chocolate and sugar; mix well and chill. Add ice cream and milk to chocolate mixture just before serving, blending well with a wire whisk. Garnish punch with whipped cream and grated chocolate. Serve immediately.

Mrs. Thomas W. Morningstar (Donna)

Wine cooler: Add spoonful of frozen concentrated punch to each glass of wine. Top with club soda.

DAILEY'S BLOODY MARY

1 tablespoon crushed caraway seed
1 tablespoon Dijon mustard
3 teaspoons celery salt
5 ounces Worcestershire sauce
1 1/2 ounces lemon juice
1/2 teaspoon white pepper
2 teaspoons black pepper
1 teaspoon garlic salt
2 drops Tabasco sauce
2 teaspoons horseradish
1 ounce beef broth
1/4 teaspoon cumin
1 can Sacramento tomato juice
1 1/2 ounces vodka
Cucumber slice

Mix all ingredients together except tomato juice, vodka and cucumber slice, in 1-quart container. In an 11-ounce salt-rimmed glass of ice, add vodka. Fill glass with mix and garnish with cucumber slice.

George Baker
Dailey's
Atlanta, Georgia

CARLOS McGEE'S BLOODY MARY

1 (No. 12) can V-8 juice
1 cup beef broth
1/2 cup Worcestershire sauce
1 tablespoon juice from can of jalapeno peppers
2 teaspoons cayenne
1 teaspoon chili powder

Mix ingredients in blender for 2 minutes. Pour into a glass with celery salt on rim (wet rim with lime). Squeeze in lime. Pour in 1 1/2 ounces vodka or tequila. Pour over ice. Garnish with peperoncini pepper.

Brian Levine
Carlos McGees
Atlanta, Georgia

TOMATO VEGETABLE JUICE

Yield: 9 quarts

10 quarts tomatoes
1/2 cup salt
1 hot pepper (optional)
1 1/2 cups celery
5 large onions

4 sweet peppers
5 cups water
1/2 cup vinegar
1 cup sugar

Cook tomatoes in their own juice and run through sieve to remove peel and seeds. Cook together the celery, onions, and peppers in the 5 cups water until tender, then run through blender. Add salt, vinegar, sugar, vegetable mixture to tomatoes and mix well. Bring to a rolling boil and put into sterilized jars and seal while hot.

Mrs. Henry Sewell (Lucy)

"I love everything that is old—old friends, old times, old manners, old books, old wine."

Burns

HOMEMADE CORDIALS

Simple Syrup: bring water to boil and stir in as much sugar as will dissolve.

Standard Syrup/Vodka Mix:

16 ounces (80-90 proof) Vodka	**1/2 cup simple syrup (or substitute light corn syrup) Thin with 1/4 cup water if necessary**

Creme de menthe

to standard syrup/Vodka mix add: 1 1/2 teaspoons oil & peppermint
1 teaspoon green food coloring

Creme de mocha (similar to Kahlua)

shake 16 ounces vodka with heaping tablespoon instant coffee
add 1/2 cup simple syrup (or corn syrup)

Orange curacao (similar to Cointreau or Triple Sec)

1 1/2 teaspoons orange oil; orange food coloring in standard syrup/vodka mix (use brandy instead of vodka for a flavor similar to Grand Marnier)

Almond liquor (similar to Amaretto)

1 1/2 teaspoons almond oil to standard syrup/vodka mix

Wrap wine glasses in cloth napkins to prevent breaking and at picnic each person will receive their glass and napkin together.

HOUSEKEEPER'S ALPHABET

APPLES—Keep in dry place, as cool as possible without freezing.
BROOMS—Hang in the cellar-way to keep soft and pliant.
CRANBERRIES—Keep under water, in cellar; change water monthly.
DISH of hot water set in oven prevents cakes, etc., from scorching.
ECONOMIZE time, health, and means, and you will never beg.
FLOUR—Keep cool, dry, and securely covered.
GLASS—Clean with a quart of water mixed with table-spoon of ammonia.
HERBS—Gather when beginning to blossom; keep in paper sacks.
INK STAINS—Wet with spirits turpentine; after three hours, rub well.
JARS—To prevent, coax "husband" to buy our Cook-Book.
KEEP an account of all supplies, with cost and date when purchased.
LOVE lightens labor.
MONEY—Count carefully when you receive change.
NUTMEGS—Prick with a pin, and if good, oil will run out.
ORANGE and LEMON PEEL—Dry, pound, and keep in corked bottles.
PARSNIPS—Keep in ground until spring.
QUICKSILVER and white of an egg destroys bedbugs.
RICE—Select large, with a clear, fresh look; old rice may have insects.
SUGAR—For general family use, the granulated is best.
TEA—Equal parts of Japan and green are as good as English breakfast.
USE a cement made of ashes, salt, and water for cracks in stove.
VARIETY is the best culinary spice.
WATCH your back yard for dirt and bones.
XANTIPPE was a scold. Don't imitate her.
YOUTH is best preserved by a cheerful temper.
ZINC-LINED sinks are better than wooden ones.
& regulate the clock by your husband's watch, and in all apportionments
of time remember the Giver.

The Dixie Cook-Book (1888)

A P P E T I Z E R S

Cold Meat and Cheese Server

APPETIZERS—HOT

APPETIZERS—COLD

CALIFORNIA GOUDA

Oven: 375°   Yield: 6 to 8 servings

1 round Gouda cheese	1 jar hot pepper jelly
1 four-roll package crescent rolls	Triscuits

Remove red wax from Gouda. Unwrap crescent rolls and pinch together seams to form two rectangles. Wrap rolls around cheese in two sheets until cheese is encrusted. Place in oven until crust is golden brown. Remove from oven and serve with pepper jelly on top. Serve hot on Triscuit Crackers.

Mrs. Jett Fisher (Carol)

CAMEMBERT SAUTÉ

1 six inch round Camembert cheese (medium soft)	4 tablespoons unsalted butter
1 egg, beaten	1/2 cup chopped green onion tops
1 cup fresh bread crumbs	

Dip the unskinned cheese round in the egg and then coat both sides with bread crumbs. Heat 2 tablespoons of the butter until it starts to brown. Over high heat brown cheese round on both sides. Remove to a heated serving plate and keep warm. Add the remaining butter to the skillet. When foamy, sauté the onions for 2 minutes. Pour over top of the cheese round and serve immediately with Carr's table wafers or plain Bremner wafers.

Mrs. Robert Teller (Nancy)

Store garlic cloves in cooking oil. They won't dry out and you can use flavored oil for cooking.

MEXICAN FUDGE

Oven: 350° for 20 minutes

Yield: 12 to 14 servings

1 (7 1/2 ounce) can Picante
sauce

3 eggs
1 pound cheese, grated

Mix sauce and eggs. Put half of the cheese in bottom of casserole dish and pour half of egg mixture over cheese. Repeat with cheese and remaining egg mixture. Bake 20 minutes at 350°.

Mrs. Bob Wiggins (Jane Tillman)

ASPARAGUS BLANKETS

Oven: 400° 10 minutes

Yield: 10 servings

1 loaf Roman Meal Bread
2 small packages of cream
cheese
1/2 pound of sharp cheddar
cheese

Butter
1/2 cup of salad dressing
1 teaspoon of salt
34 asparagus spears

Cut off crust of bread from the entire loaf. Mix all of the remaining ingredients together except the asparagus spears. Spread mixture on each piece of bread. Put 1 or 2 asparagus spears on each piece and roll up corner to corner. Secure with a toothpick. Place on a cookie sheet and brush with melted butter. Bake about 10 minutes at 400° and serve hot.

Mrs. Frank Parham (Jackie Cordle)
Ringgold, Georgia

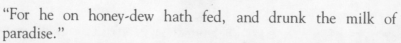

"For he on honey-dew hath fed, and drunk the milk of paradise."

Samuel Taylor Coleridge

SPINACH BALLS

Oven: 350° 20 minutes   Yield: 4 dozen

4 eggs
2 packages (10 ounce)
  chopped spinach
1/2 small chopped onion
3/4 cup melted margarine

1/2 cup grated parmesan
  cheese
1 cup grated cheddar cheese
1/2 teaspoon garlic salt
2 cups Pepperidge Farm
  stuffing mix

Slightly beat eggs. Add remaining ingredients and mix thoroughly. Shape into balls the size of walnuts. Refrigerate 30 minutes before baking. Place on ungreased cookie sheet. Bake at 350° for 20 minutes. Can be frozen after baking.

Mary Lynn Hall

HOT BROCCOLI DIP

2 10 ounce package frozen
  chopped broccoli
2 rolls garlic cheese (Kraft)
2 8 ounce cream cheese
3 cups celery—chopped

2 medium onions
1 stick butter
2 cans cream mushroom soup
2 small packages slivered
  almonds

Sauté onions and celery in butter. Add two cheeses and soup and melt together. Stir in cooked and drained broccoli. Add almonds. Serve hot with crackers. Makes 1 1/2–2 quarts.

Mrs. Dennis McEntire (Sally)

Chafing Dish with Burner

25

STUFFED MUSHROOMS

Oven: 500° 8 to 10 minutes

1 pound fresh mushrooms
8 ounce cream cheese,
  softened

1/2 cup grated Parmesan
  cheese
1 tablespoon garlic salt

Preheat oven to 500°. Wash mushrooms, remove and discard stems. Place on paper towel to dry. Mix cheeses and garlic salt until smooth and creamy. Add more garlic salt to taste if necessary. Fill mushrooms with heaping mixture. Place in preheated oven for about 8 to 10 minutes or until cheese bubbles. Serve immediately.

Mrs. Joe Almon, Jr. (Deena)

QUICK STUFFED MUSHROOMS
Substitute 6 ounces cream cheese mixed with 1 packet of ranch dressing
for a delicious variation

Oven: 350° 15 minutes   Yield: 4 servings

12 medium fresh mushrooms
1/4 cup butter, melted

1 (5 ounce) Boursin, Tarter
  or Rondele cheese with
  herbs and garlic

Preheat oven to 350°. Clean mushrooms and remove stems. Brush outside of caps with melted butter. Fill caps with cheese. Arrange on small baking sheet and bake about 15 minutes.

Mrs. Scott Arrowsmith (Sandey)

SAUSAGE STUFFED MUSHROOMS

Oven: Preheat to 350°

1 lb. mushroom caps (raw)   1/4 cup butter
1 lb. sausage   Parmesan cheese
1 8 oz. cream cheese

Lightly sauté caps in butter. Arrange on cookie sheet and set aside. Brown sausage and drain off grease. Mix sausage and cream cheese until smooth. Fill mushroom caps. Sprinkle with Parmesan cheese. Bake for 10 minutes. (May be made a day before and refrigerated.)

Mrs. Charles V. Slomka (Tricia)

SPINACH STUFFED MUSHROOMS

Oven: 350° 15 minutes   Yield: 4 to 6 servings

15 large mushrooms   1/2 package frozen chopped
8 ounce package cream cheese   spinach (thawed and
   softened   squeezed dry)
                               2 tablespoons melted butter

Remove stems. Mix cream cheese and spinach. Season to taste with salt and pepper (may add a dash of onion powder to taste). Spoon into mushroom tops mounding slightly. Place in glass baking dish that has been lightly coated with melted butter. Bake at 350° for 15 minutes.

Mrs. Scott Arrowsmith (Sandey)

SWEET & SOUR MEATBALLS
Great for parties

Yield: 25 to 30 servings

Meatballs:

1 1/2 lbs. ground chuck
2/3 cup bread crumbs
1/2 cup chopped onion
2/3 cup evaporated milk

1 teaspoon salt
Flour
Oil

Sauce:

1 can pineapple chunk (lg.)
1 cup pineapple juice
1/2 cup vinegar
1/2 cup brown sugar
2 tablespoons soy sauce

2 tablespoons corn starch
2 tablespoons lemon juice
1 cup green pepper strips
1 can mandarin oranges
1 small jar pimento

Mix meatball ingredients together and make into balls. Roll in flour and brown in oil. Pour off excess fat. Mix sauce ingredients, with exception of pepper, pineapple and oranges. Stir in large skillet until thick. Add pepper and fruits and simmer 15 minutes. Pour sauce over meatballs and serve warm.

Mrs. Thomas W. Morningstar (Donna)
Sharpsburg, Georgia

Covered Chafing Dish

WATER CHESTNUTS & BACON

Oven: 350° 15 minutes   Serves: 10

1 can whole or sliced water   1/2 cup brown sugar
   chestnuts (8 ounce)   1/2 cup teriyaki sauce
2 cups orange juice   Bacon

Mix orange juice, brown sugar, and teriyaki sauce. Pour over water chestnuts and marinate for 4 hours in refrigerator. Broil bacon until soft. Cut in strips long enough to wrap around water chestnuts. Bake for 15 minutes at 350° or until bacon is brown.

Mrs. Linda Stone
Moreland, Georgia

HOT SWISS CANAPÉS

Oven: Broil 4 to 5 minutes   Yield: 2 dozen

3 egg whites   1/4 cup chopped green onions
1 1/2 cups (6 ounces) Swiss   1/2 teaspoon salt
   cheese, shredded   1/8 teaspoon pepper
3 slices uncooked bacon,   24 slices party rye bread
   chopped

Beat egg whites (at room temperature) until stiff peaks form; fold in Swiss cheese, bacon, green pepper, green onions, salt, and pepper.

Spread about 1 tablespoon mixture on each bread slice. Place on baking sheets, broil 4 to 5 inches from heat about 5 minutes or until bacon cooks. Serve immediately.

Mrs. Thomas W. Morningstar (Donna)
Sharpsburg, Georgia

WIENIE BITS

Oven: 350° 1 hour   Yield: 20 servings

1 package ten regular wieners   1 pound regular sliced bacon
**   (good brand)   Granulated brown sugar**

Cut each wiener into 4 pieces. Cut each bacon slice into 3 pieces. Wrap bacon around each wiener piece. Place in 9x9x2 pan so they fit snugly so bacon stays wrapped. Cover with brown sugar. Bake uncovered for one hour. Pour off grease and serve in chafing dish with toothpicks.

Mrs. Charles Cobb (Marian)
Rockford, Illinois

SPICY SESAME CHICKEN WINGS
Very Spicy!

Oven: 400° for 40 to 50 minutes   Yield: 12 servings

12 chicken wings (about 2   1/2 teaspoon crushed red
**   pounds), separated at joints   pepper**
4 cups soy sauce   1 large egg, beaten
2-inch piece peeled   1/2 cup Italian bread crumbs
**   gingerroot, minced   1/3 cup sesame seeds**
2 small cloves garlic, minced   1/4 cup butter or margarine,
1/4 teaspoon freshly ground   melted
**   black pepper**

Place chicken in large non-metal bowl. Process soy sauce, ginger and garlic in blender or food processor until smooth. Pour over chicken. Sprinkle with black and red pepper. Cover with plastic wrap and refrigerate at least 30 minutes. Pour beaten egg over wings and mix well. Mix bread crumbs and sesame seeds in a pie plate. Coat wings with crumb mixture, pressing firmly. Arrange on lightly oiled cookie sheet. Drizzle with butter. Bake in preheated 400° oven for 40 to 50 minutes until well-browned and crisp. (NOTE: May be baked ahead and frozen. Reheat straight from freezer in 350° oven for 30 minutes.)

Robert Lewis Jarrell
Atlanta, Georgia

PICO DE GALLO
FRESH SALSA

1/2 onion	4 to 5 tomatoes, chopped
1 to 2 cloves minced garlic	Chopped cilantro—to taste
4 to 5 chilies, serrano or	
jalapeno (fresh)	

Process ingredients, except tomato and cilantro, in food processor or blender. Add tomatoes and cilantro. Blend for a second, (you want it to be chunky). Salt to taste.

Serve with tortilla chips or use in recipes in place of canned salsa.

Mrs. Hugh Heflin (Julia Berry)

CREAM CHEESE TORTILLAS WITH PICO DE GALLO

Spread softened cream cheese on flour tortillas. Roll up and slice 1/2 to 1 inch thick. Top with fresh salsa. Serve with toothpicks.

Mrs. Hugh Heflin (Julia Berry)

Give me books, fruit, French wine and fine weather, and a little music out of doors, played by someone I do not know.

John Keats

PARTY GUACAMOLE

3 mashed avocados
Juice of one lemon
Garlic salt to taste
3/4 jar of bacon bits
8 green onions, chopped
2 tablespoons of cilantro

2 large tomatoes, chopped
1 (8 ounce) sour cream (or less)
Mild cheddar cheese
Monterey Jack cheese
1 large bag tortilla chips

Layer the ingredients as follows: mix mashed avocados with lemon juice and garlic salt. Spread in bottom of round dish. Sprinkle bacon bits over avocado mixture. Layer in order listed the next 4 ingredients. Top with grated cheddar cheese and Monterey Jack cheese. Serve with tortilla chips.

Mrs. Richard James (Sara)

ASPARAGUS MOLD

1 1/2 package plain gelatin
1/4 cup cold water
1 can cream of asparagus soup
1 (8 oz.) cream cheese
3/4 cup chopped celery

1 jar chopped pimiento (lg.)
3/4 cup chopped onion
1 cup mayonnaise
1/8 teaspoon red pepper
Green food coloring

Add gelatin to water and let set 5 minutes. Heat soup to almost boiling (but *do not boil*). Add cream cheese and stir until melted. Add gelatin to hot soup mixture and cool. Add celery, pimiento, onions, mayonnaise and red pepper. Add a few drops of food coloring until desired color. Stir well. Pour in 1 quart salad mold and refrigerate. Unmold and serve with crackers.

Mrs. Sam O. Candler (Betsy)
Sharpsburg, Georgia

MARINATED MUSHROOMS

2 pounds mushrooms
1/2 teaspoon salt
1/2 cup juice (from
   mushrooms)
1/2 cup apple cider vinegar
1/4 cup white wine
1 tablespoon dry minced
   onion
1/2 teaspoon lemon pepper

1/2 teaspoon dry minced
   garlic
1/2 teaspoon sugar
1/2 teaspoon thyme
1/2 teaspoon celery salt
1/4 teaspoon tarragon
3 drops Tabasco
2 bay leaves

Cook mushrooms in pan by putting in pan and sprinkling with salt. (Reserve juice from cooked mushrooms). Cover and cook over medium heat for 11 to 12 minutes. Drain. Reserve juice. Place all other ingredients in pan and heat to boiling. Pour over mushrooms in jar. Let cool. Cover and refrigerate for 24 hours.

Optional serving: Peel outer leaves of cabbage back and use to surround head. Using toothpicks, fasten mushrooms to cabbage, covering tip in circular fashion. Looks very festive and fancy.

Margaret Ann Watkins
Atlanta, Georgia

STUFFED CELERY FILLING

2 (8 ounce) packages cream
   cheese
1 tablespoon mayonnaise

3 drops lemon juice
3 drops worcestershire sauce
1 tablespoon grated onion

Soften cream cheese with mayonnaise. Use as much mayonnaise as needed to soften cream cheese—approximately 1 tablespoon. Add lemon juice, worcestershire sauce, and grated onion to taste (all ingredients may vary according to taste). Stuff celery.

Mrs. Duke Blackburn, Jr. (Lynn)

MUSHROOM PATE

Yield: 4 to 6 servings

1 pound fresh mushrooms
1/2 stick butter
1 tablespoon lemon juice
1 tablespoon Madeira or
  sherry (optional)
1/8 teaspoon cayenne pepper

1/4 teaspoon tarragon vinegar
1/8 teaspoon salt
1 stick butter, softened
2 eggs, scrambled
4 tablespoons Parmesan
  cheese

Slice mushrooms and sauté in 1/2 stick of butter. Add lemon juice. Cook for 5 minutes, shaking pan often. Puree mushrooms and their juice in a blender or food processor. Cool slightly. Add seasonings and softened stick of butter. Cook eggs in a little butter. Add eggs and cheese to mushroom mixture. Mix well, put in a crock and refrigerate. Serve on melba toast rounds.

Mrs. Scott Arrowsmith (Sandey)

CHEDDAR-CHUTNEY PATÉ

Yield: 10 to 12 servings

1 (8 ounce) bucket cold pack
  cheddar, room temperature
6 ounces Philadelphia cream
  cheese, softened
2 teaspoons curry powder

2 tablespoons dry sherry
1 bottle Major Grey's
  Chutney
Chives
Wheat Thins

Whip cheddar, cream cheese, curry and sherry with beater. Put in low silver bowl. Refrigerate overnight. Take out to soften a few hours before party. Cover with chutney. Sprinkle chives over top. Serve with Wheat Thins.

Mrs. Robert Teller (Nancy)

CHEESE AND NUT PÂTÉ

1 8 oz. cream cheese
1 1-lb. extra sharp cheddar
cheese (grated)
1 8 oz. roquefort cheese (bleu)

Garlic powder—optional (or 2
cloves fresh garlic, crushed)
Chopped nuts and parsley
flakes

Grate cheddar cheese and combine cream cheese and roquefort cheese together. Have all three cheeses at room temp. After mixing these together along with garlic, roll into two balls and cover with nuts and parsley flakes. Wrap in saran paper to keep fresh, or can be frozen. Delicious with your favorite cracker!

Mrs. Donald Tolbert (Janie)

CHEDDAR CHEESE BALL

16 oz. sharp cheddar cheese
8 oz. cream cheese
2 tablespoons lemon juice
Dash of red pepper
1/2 cup chopped pecans

1/2 teaspoon garlic salt (or
less)
Paprika
1/2 cup chopped pecans
(optional)

Grate cheddar cheese and let both cheeses come to room temperature. Mix all ingredients together and form into ball. Roll ball in paprika and, if desired, 1/2 cup chopped pecans. Serve with crackers.

Mrs. Tom Carson (Nancy)

NIPPY RUM SPREAD

Yield: 1 cup

9 oz. cream cheese
1/4 cup rum
1 teaspoon prepared mustard

1 teaspoon prepared
horseradish
1 tablespoon caraway seed

Soften cheese at room temperature and blend with rum, mustard, horseradish and caraway seed. Chill until ready to serve. Serve on assorted crackers.

Mrs. L. Stephen Mitchell (Linda)

35

VICKIE'S CHEESE BALLS

Yield: 12 to 14 servings

2 (8 ounce) packages cream
  cheese
1/2 jar dried beef (cut up
  very fine)
1/2 large jar mushrooms

1/2 can chopped ripe olives
1/2 bundle green chives
  (chopped)
1 teaspoon Accent
Triscuits

Soften cream cheese. Add remaining ingredients. Form into ball and refrigerate. Serve with Triscuits.

Mrs. Robert Cordle (Mitzi)

TROPICAL CHEESE BALL

2 (8 ounce) cream cheese
1 small can crushed
  pineapple, drained
1/4 cup bell pepper, chopped
  fine

2 tablespoons minced onions
1 tablespoon seasoned salt
2 cups grated pecans

Mix all ingredients, except 1 cup of the grated pecans. Form into one or two balls. Roll in remaining cup of grated pecans.

Mrs. W.L. Hartley (Laura)
Luthersville, Georgia

THREE CHEESE LOGS
OR 1 LARGE CHEESE BALL

3 large (8 oz.) packages cream
  cheese
2 teaspoons liquid smoke
7 scallions—tops and all
  chopped finely

2 small or 1 large Armour
  Dried Beef—finely chopped
Pecans—chopped

Mix together and form into 3 logs. Roll each log in chopped nuts or parsley. You can add 1/2 cup chopped pecans to cheese mixture before forming logs.

Mrs. Jimmy Hutchinson (Jane)

PERNOD CHEESE DIP

Yield: 4 1/2 cups

3 (8 ounce) cream cheese,
 room temperature
1 1/2 tablespoons Pernod
1/2 cup small curd cottage
 cheese

1/4 cup snipped fresh chives
1/4 cup hulled sunflower
 seeds, toasted
1 tablespoon caraway seeds

Cream together cream cheese and Pernod. Stir in remaining ingredients and mix well. Pack dip into a bowl or crock and chill at least one hour.

Mrs. William M. Berry, III (Anne Jarrell)

ELM STREET SCHOOL CHEESE WAFERS

Oven: 350° for 10 to 12 minutes   Yield: 8 dozen

8 cups flour
3 tablespoons red pepper
3 teaspoons salt

2 1/2 pounds sharp cheddar
 cheese, grated
1 1/2 pounds butter
2 cups Rice Krispies

Mix all ingredients, except Rice Krispies, together. Then add Rice Krispies, mixing lightly. Drop by tablespoons onto greased cookie sheet and bake in 350° oven until very lightly browned, approximately 10 to 12 minutes.

Mrs. Eugene Jackson (Ruth)
Elm Street School

"I do like a little bit of butter to my bread."
A.A. Milne

CHEESE PENNIES

Oven: Preheat to 400°   Yield: 5 dozen

1/3 cup margarine, softened
1/2 lb sharp cheddar cheese,
  grated

1 cup sifted plain flour
2 or 3 tablespoons dry Lipton
  onion soup mix

Combine margarine and cheese. Mix with flour and soup mix and blend until dough form. Divide into 2 long log-type rolls and roll in wax paper. Refrigerate until firm. Slice in 1/4" thick slices and bake on ungreased cookie sheet until lightly brown (about 10 minutes; *do not overbake*).

Elaine Christopher

AVOCADO, EGG, CAVIAR
3-LAYERED HORS D'OEUVRE
Easy and can be made the morning before and chilled in refrigerator

1 large avocado
1/2 teaspoon lemon juice
6 hard boiled eggs, grated
3 tablespoons mayonnaise

1 (3 1/2 ounce) jar black
  caviar
Fresh parsley
Bremner wafers or crackers

Mash avocado and add lemon juice. Spread in Pyrex pie pan for first layer. Mix grated eggs and mayonnaise. Spread on top of avocado to make second layer. Spread caviar on top of eggs to make third layer. Garnish with fresh parsley. Serve with Bremner wafers or crackers.

Mrs. Minerva Cole Woodroof

Candle Snuffer

CRABMEAT OR SHRIMP SPREAD

1 8 oz. cream cheese
1 8 oz. jar Heinz cocktail
  sauce
2 cans Orleans crabmeat

1 medium lemon
large box of Triscuits
Parsley (optional)

Spread cream cheese thinly on a large serving platter. Next spread cocktail sauce on top of cream cheese. Squeeze any excess water out of crabmeat and sprinkle over cocktail sauce. Cut lemon in half and squeeze juice on top of crabmeat. Garnish with parsley, if desired, and serve with crackers. (Shrimp may be substituted for crabmeat.)

Mrs. Peter Gosch (Lisa)

SMOKED OYSTER SPREAD

1 (8-ounce) cream cheese
2 tablespoons mayonnaise
1 tin smoked oysters
  (chopped)

3/4 cup stuffed green olives
  (sliced)
1/2 teaspoon lemon juice
Dash garlic salt

Soften cream cheese and cream well with mayonnaise and lemon juice. Add oysters, olives, and garlic salt. Form into a ball, cake, or roll and garnish with olives. Chill. Serve as a spread on crackers.

Mrs. Charles V. Slomka (Tricia)

SEASONED OYSTER CRACKERS

1 box oyster crackers
4 ounce dry package ranch
  dressing

1 cup vegetable oil
1 tablespoon dill

Assemble all ingredients. Turn every few hours with a spoon until all oil is absorbed. Takes about 24 hours. Store in sealed container.

Mrs. Tom Carson (Nancy)

CAVIAR MOUSSE

Yield: 12 to 15

6 large eggs, hard boiled
1 small onion, grated
1 cup mayonnaise
1 envelope Knox gelatin
1 teaspoon worcestershire sauce

2 tablespoons lemon juice
2 tablespoons sherry
1 teaspoon anchovy paste (or more to taste)
1 (3 1/2 ounce) jar caviar

In double boiler, dissolve gelatin in sherry, lemon and worcestershire. Put eggs in blender or food processor and chop fine. Add mayonnaise and grated onion. Add anchovy paste to double boiler mixture. Add double boiler mix to egg mix. Fold in caviar. Pour into greased mold. Refrigerate 1 hour or more. Unmold. Serve.

Mrs. Robert Teller (Nancy)

GEORGIA CAVIAR
Also good used as side dish

Yield: 24 servings

1 (16 ounce) bag dry blackeye peas
1 (2 ounce) jar pimiento, chopped
1 large bell pepper, chopped

3 jalapeno peppers (or to taste)
7 or 8 spring onions, chopped
1 large onion, chopped
1 large bottle Italian dressing

Soak and cook dry peas. Rinse in cold water. Mix with remaining ingredients and refrigerate overnight. Serve with large corn chips.

Sarah Johnson

Pickle Fork

FROSTED SANDWICH LOAF

Yield: 24 to 36 servings

Ham-pickle filling (below)
Chicken salad filling (below)
Curried egg filling (below)
Peeled tomatoes
1 lb. 13 oz. loaf unsliced
    bread

butter or margarine
2 tablespoons mayonnaise
2 (8 ounce) packages cream
    cheese
1/4 cup mayonnaise
2 tablespoons light cream

Prepare fillings, slice tomatoes, chill. Cut crust from bread. Lay loaf on its side. Cut into 5 even slices. Spread 4 slices with butter or margarine. Spread filling on 3 slices, arrange tomato slices on fourth. Spread tomatoes with 2 tablespoons mayonnaise. Stack slices, top with fifth slice of bread. Mix cream cheese, 1/4 cup mayonnaise and cream until smooth. Spread mixture on top and sides of loaf. Chill thoroughly. Garnish with sieved hard cooked egg yolks if desired. (Any type filling can be substituted, i.e., shrimp salad, tuna, crab.)

HAM-PICKLE FILLING:
3 cans deviled ham

1/4 cup sour pickles chopped

CHICKEN SALAD FILLING:
1/3 cup mayonnaise
1 teaspoon grated onion
1 teaspoon lemon juice
1/2 teaspoon salt

1 cup chopped cooked chicken
1/3 cup chopped celery
3 tablespoons chopped parsley
Dash of pepper

Mix all ingredients.

CURRIED EGG FILLING:
3 hard boiled eggs, finely
    chopped
1/4 cup mayonnaise
1 teaspoon prepared mustard

1 teaspoon grated onion
1/2 teaspoon curry powder
1/2 teaspoon salt
Dash of pepper

Mix all ingredients.

Mrs. Jimmy Hutchinson, Jr. (Jane)

41

DAINTY VEGETABLE PIZZA

Oven: As directed on package   Yield: 35 2-inch pieces

1 roll crescent rolls
1 (8 ounce) cream cheese,
  room temperature
1/3 cup mayonnaise
1/2 teaspoon dill weed

1/4 teaspoon garlic powder
1 teaspoon minced onion
Radishes, celery, carrots, and
  green peppers, finely
  chopped

Press crescent rolls into a jelly roll pan. Bake as directed on package, until golden brown. Cool. Mix remaining ingredients, except vegetables, and spread on cooled crust. Top with chopped vegetables, only covering the cream cheese lightly, allowing some of it to show. Cut in very small squares. (You may use any kind of fresh vegetable, i.e., broccoli, cauliflower, etc.)

Mrs. David Kinrade (Joan)

LITTLE LINKS IN ORIENTAL SAUCE

Yield: 64 appetizers

1 cup brown sugar
3 tablespoons plain flour
2 teaspoons dry mustard
1 cup pineapple juice
1/2 cup apple cider vinegar

1 1/2 teaspoons soy sauce
1 pound little wieners
1 pound cocktail smoked
  sausages

Combine brown sugar, flour and mustard in saucepan. Add pineapple juice, vinegar and soy sauce. Heat to boiling, stirring constantly. Boil 1 minute and stir in wieners and sausages. Cook slowly for 5 minutes, or until heated through. Keep warm over low heat in chafing dish. Use wooden picks for serving.

SPICED PECANS

1 pound pecan halves
1/4 cup water
1 teaspoon cinnamon
1 teaspoon salt

1/2 teaspoon nutmeg
1 teaspoon vanilla
1 cup sugar

Mix all ingredients in a black iron skillet and stir over medium heat until the sugar melts. Cover pecans with syrup. Be careful not to burn.

These are a great gift idea and Christmas treat.

Mrs. Sam Candler (Betsy)
Sharpsburg, Georgia

FRESH FRUIT DIP

Yield: 6 to 8 servings

1 to 2 cups of sour cream or
  8 oz. softened cream cheese

Crushed macaroon cookies
Lemon juice

You may use sour cream alone or a combination of sour cream and cream cheese. Mix with crushed macaroon cookies and add a little bit of lemon juice to enhance the flavor.

Serve with bite-sized fresh fruit, such as strawberries or seedless grapes. Particularly pretty using red and green apple slices with the dip in the center of the platter.

Mrs. Scott Arrowsmith (Sandey)

A slamming of oven doors, and the rattle and clatter of dishes, tire and bewilder everybody about the house. Those who accomplish much in housekeeping—and the same is true of every other walk in life—are the quiet workers.

The Dixie Cook-Book (1888)

RIO GRANDE DIP

Oven: 375°

8 ounce package cream cheese
1 can Cassleberry Hot Dog
    Chili
1 cup hot salsa
Black olives

Green onions
Sliced jalapeno peppers
1 package mild cheddar
    cheese
1 package monterey cheese

Spread cream cheese on bottom of small casserole dish. Spread hot dog chili on top, add hot salsa. Top with black olives, green onions, jalapeno peppers and cheeses. Bake til cheese melts. Serve with chips.

OPTION: Add sour cream, lettuce and tomatoes for topping after you take it out of the oven.

Ms. Sandra B. Watson
St. Petersburg, Florida

'Come in good time, my dear Dutchess,' said Rivvy's letter, 'and we will have something so very nice. I am baking it in a pie-dish—a pie-dish with a pink rim. You never tasted anything so good! And **you** shall eat it all! I will eat muffins!

Beatrix Potter

B R E A D S &

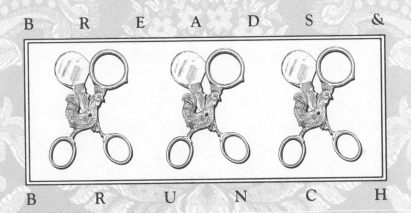

B R U N C H

Egg Cutter

Used to cut the end from a soft boiled egg,
so that it can be eaten from the shell.

BREADS

BRUNCH

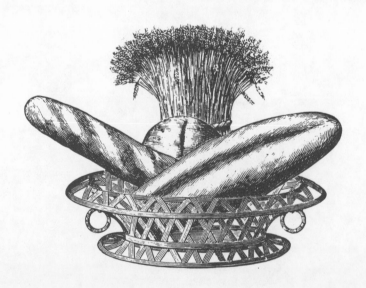

JANE'S HOMEMADE BISCUIT MIX
Use like any biscuit mix, such as Bisquick

Oven: 250° 5 minutes

9 cups all purpose flour
1/3 cup baking powder
1 tablespoon salt
2 teaspoons cream of tartar

4 tablespoons sugar
1 cup non-fat dry milk
2 cups shortening which does
   not require refrigeration

Stir together flour, baking powder, salt, cream of tartar, sugar, and dry milk thoroughly, in large bowl or pan. (Mix may be made in heavy sterilized paper grocery bag. Sanitize by placing folded bag in a preheated, 250° oven for 5 minutes.) Cut in shortening with pastry blender or two knives or clean hands until mixture looks like coarse corn meal. Store in covered containers at room temperature. To measure the mix, pile it lightly into a cup and level off with a spatula.

For whole wheat master mix use 5 cups plain flour and four cups whole wheat flour.

Mrs. Don Tomlinson (Jane)
Asheville, North Carolina

QUICK MUFFINS

Oven: 350° 12 to 15 minutes   Yield: 6 muffins

2 cups self-rising flour
1 cup milk

1/2 cup mayonnaise

Mix all ingredients. Spoon into greased muffin pan. Bake at 350° for 12 to 15 minutes or until golden brown.

Mrs. L. Stephen Mitchell (Linda)

JANE'S COFFEE CAKE

Oven: 350° 20 to 25 minutes   Yield: 30 squares

4 cups Bisquick (or Jane's
    Homemade Biscuit Mix)
1/2 cup sugar
1/4 cup butter or margarine,
    melted

1/2 cup milk
1 teaspoon vanilla
3 eggs
1 (21 ounce) can fruit pie
    filling, any flavor

Glaze:

1 cup powdered sugar   1 to 2 tablespoons milk

Mix all ingredients except pie filling and glaze. Beat well for 30 seconds. Spread 2/3 of batter in greased 10x15 jelly roll pan. Spread pie filling over batter. Drop remaining batter by tablespoons onto pie filling. Bake 20 to 25 minutes at 350° until light brown. Make glaze by mixing glaze ingredients until smooth. Drizzle over coffee cake. Cool slightly, then cut into squares.

Mrs. Don Tomlinson (Jane)
Asheville, North Carolina

RUTH'S BUTTER ORANGE CRESCENT ROLLS

Oven: 375° 11 to 15 minutes   Yield: 24 rolls

Rind of 1 orange
1/2 cup sugar

3 packages Pillsbury crescent
    rolls
Melted butter

Combine orange rind and sugar. Let sit overnight. When ready to serve, unroll dough from package, but do not separate. Brush liberally with melted butter. Measure 1 teaspoon of orange-sugar mixture for each triangle. Brush mixture over surface, one triangle at a time. Cut apart and roll as directed on package for jelly roll. Do not brush top with egg white. Bake at 375° for 11 to 15 minutes. Do not over bake.

Hint: When grating orange, use light touch to obtain only zest of orange. The white part of rind is bitter.

Mrs. Scott Arrowsmith (Sandey)

AUNT MARY'S ORANGE BREAD

Oven: 350° 1 hour   Yield: 1 loaf

Grated peel of 4 oranges
1 1/2 cups sugar
2 eggs
1 cup milk
3 1/4 cups flour

3 teaspoons baking powder
2 tablespoons melted fat
1/2 teaspoon salt
Nuts (optional)

Preheat oven to 350°. Boil orange peel in water for 5 minutes. Pour off water. Add 1/2 cup sugar and cook until thick. Cool. Mix remaining ingredients. Add nuts if desired. Mix in orange peel mixture. Pour into a loaf pan and bake at 350° for one hour or until golden brown. Test with knife until comes out clean. Can double recipe.

Substitution: Can be baked in mini loaves, but shorten cooking time until golden brown and done inside.

Mrs. Scott Arrowsmith (Sandey)

ORANGE MUFFINS
Delicious made ahead & frozen

Oven: 375° 15 minutes   Yield: 3 dozen

Batter:

2 cups plain flour
1 teaspoon baking soda
1 stick butter
1 cup sugar

2 eggs
3/4 cup buttermilk
1 cup golden raisins
1 cup chopped pecans

Glaze:

1 cup sugar

Juice and rind of 2 oranges
and 1 lemon

Sift flour and soda together. Cream butter, sugar and eggs. Then add flour and milk together. Add raisins and pecans. Pour in small muffin pan and bake for 15 minutes. Stir glaze ingredients together. Dip muffins while hot.

Betty Stapler

49

BUTTER CINNAMON ROLLS

Oven: 425° 15 minutes   Yield: 12 rolls

1/4 cup cold butter or
  margarine
2 1/2 cups Bisquick (or Jane's
  Homemade Biscuit Mix)
1/2 cup milk

1 egg
2 tablespoons butter or
  margarine, softened
3 tablespoons sugar
1 1/4 teaspoons cinnamon

Glaze:

1 cup 4X sugar   1 to 2 tablespoons milk

Heat oven to 425°. Grease 8" sqaure pan. Cut cold butter into 1/4" cubes. Toss baking mix and cubes until coated. Mix milk and egg together and stir into butter mixture. Turn dough onto cloth covered board that has been dusted with flour; roll to coat dough. Fold and knead 10 times. Shape into a 15x8 rectangle. Spread with soft butter. Mix sugar and cinnamon and sprinkle over dough. Roll up into jelly roll, beginning with 15-inch side. Cut into 12 slices with a sharp knife. Place in pan side by side. Bake until golden, about 15 minutes. Cool for 15 minutes. Make glaze by mixing ingredients until smooth. Drizzle cinnamon rolls with glaze.

Mrs. Don Tomlinson (Jane)
Asheville, North Carolina

CHEESE MUFFINS
For Carraway Cheese Muffins: add 2 tablespoons carraway seeds

Oven: 450° for 10 minutes   Yield: 4 dozen muffins (small)

2 cups Bisquick
1/2 cup butter or margarine,
  melted

1 (8 ounce) sour cream
1/2 cup (about 2 ounces)
  cheddar cheese, shredded

Combine all ingredients, mixing well. Spoon into small muffin tins, filling one-half full. Bake at 450° for about 10 minutes.

Mrs. Stanley Lanier (Debbie)

OAT BRAN MUFFINS
No fat or cholesterol

Oven: 425° 12 to 15 minutes   Yield: 12 muffins

3 egg whites
1 cup fruit juice
1/2 cup maple syrup or honey
2 1/2 cups oat bran

1/2 cup oatmeal
1 tablespoon baking powder
1/2 teaspoon salt (optional)
1/2 cup dried fruit, chopped

In food processor (or mixer) process egg whites until foamy. Add juice and syrup or honey. Pulse until blended. In separate bowl, stir together oat bran, oatmeal, and baking powder (and salt if used). Add to liquid mixture, along with fruit, and pulse once until just moistened. Divide equally between 12 oiled muffin cups. Bake at 425° for 12 to 15 minutes.

Variations: For Apricot Honey Oat Bran Muffins, use chopped apricots, apricot nectar and honey. For Maple Prune Oat Bran Muffins use chopped prunes, prune juice and maple syrup.
Mrs. William M. Berry, III (Anne Jarrell)

HUSHPUPPIES

Yield: 12 to 16

1 cup white corn meal
1/3 cup flour
1 1/2 teaspoons baking powder
1 1/2 teaspoons sugar

1 1/4 teaspoons salt
1 teaspoon red pepper
1 onion, finely chopped
1 egg
3/4 cup milk

Mix dry ingredients and onion. Mix together beaten egg and milk. Add to dry ingredients. (Add more milk, if necessary, to make a very thick but smooth mixture.) Drop by tablespoon into deep hot oil to fry. Turn to brown evenly. (It's good to cook them in fish grease after fish is cooked.)
Mrs. Sam O. Candler (Betsy)
Sharpsburg, Georgia

BLUEBERRY MUFFINS

Oven: 375° 15 to 20 minutes   Yield: 2 1/2 dozen

1/2 cup shortening
1 cup sugar
3 eggs
3 cups flour

3 heaping teaspoons baking
  powder
1 teaspoon salt
1 cup milk
1 can blueberries, drained

Cream shortening and sugar with electric mixer until fluffy. Add eggs one at a time, beating well after each. Sift together flour, baking powder, salt. Add dry ingredients to mixture (beating as you go) alternately with milk. When blended, fold in drained blueberries. Mixture will be stiff. Pour in greased or lined muffin tins. Bake 375° for 15 to 20 minutes.

*Mixture will keep in the refrigerator 2 to 3 weeks. (If mixture seems a little soupy or flat after several days—add a little baking powder.)

VARIATION: Omit blueberries. Substitute 1 cup chopped pecans and add 3 teaspoons cinnamon. (Without the blueberries, this is a basic muffin batter to which just about anything can be added.)

Mrs. Delia T. Crouch

"The rule is jam tomorrow and jam yesterday, but never jam today."

Lewis Carroll

TASTY AND QUICK APPLE BREAD

Oven: 350° 1 hour 15 minutes   Yield: 1 loaf

2 cups self-rising flour
1/3 cup sugar
2 eggs, slightly beaten
1/2 cup vegetable oil
1 3/4 cup fresh apples (like

Granny Smith), shredded
in food processor
1/2 cup sharp cheddar cheese,
grated in food processor

Combine flour and sugar in large mixing bowl. Combine remaining ingredients and add all at once to flour mixture. Stir only enough to moisten flour. Batter will be thick and lumpy. Pour into greased and floured loaf pan and bake for 1 hour and 15 minutes. Remove from pan to cool before slicing.

Emily Parrott

YEAST DONUTS

Yield: 5 dozen

6 egg yolks
1/2 pound butter
6 tablespoons sugar
8 cups flour
2 teaspoons salt

2 ounces yeast (put in a little
warm water)
2 large cans Pet milk
2 teaspoons vanilla

Icing:

1 pound powdered sugar
Teaspoon vanilla

Water

Mix donut ingredients together. Roll out and cut with donut cutter. Put on cookie sheet and let rise. Cook in deep fryer or skillet, turning once. Place on paper towel to drain. Mix icing ingredients together until thin. Dip donuts in icing and drain in collander.

Ruby Reeves
Elm Street School

MRS. WIDMER'S DANISH PUFF

Oven: 350° 1 hour   Yield: 4 to 6 servings

1 cup sifted flour   **2 tablespoons water**
1/2 cup margarine

Cut margarine into flour as for pie crust. Sprinkle with water and mix with fork. Round into ball and divide in half. With floured hands pat into two strips 12x3 inches and place 3 inches apart on an ungreased baking sheet.

1/2 cup margarine   **1 cup sifted flour**
1 cup water   **3 eggs, room temperature**
1 teaspoon almond flavoring

Mix margarine and water in a saucepan. Bring to a boil and add almond flavoring. Remove from heat. Have 1 cup flour already measured out and have eggs at room temperature and ready to add. Stir in flour at once. When smooth and thick add eggs one at a time, beating smooth after each. (If mixture begins to get thin, put back on heat for a few seconds and it will thicken again.) Spread half the mixture on each strip of pastry. Bake at 350° for one hour until crisp and golden brown.

Frost with confectionery icing flavored with almond extract. Decorate with slivered almonds and cherries.

Mrs. Richard Byers (Mary Ann)

Your husband may admire your grace and ease in society, your wit, your school-day accomplishments of music and painting, but all in perfection will not atone for an ill-ordered kitchen, sour bread, muddy coffee, tough meats, unpalatable vegetables, indigestible pastry, and the whole train of horrors that result from bad housekeeping.

The Dixie Cook-Book (1888)

HUN'S SOUR CREAM COFFEE CAKE

Oven: 350° for 55 minutes   Yield: 1 tube cake

2 sticks butter, room
  temperature
2 cups sugar
1 teaspoon vanilla
1/4 teaspoon salt
2 teaspoons baking powder

1 teaspoon almond or lemon
  extract
2 eggs
2 1/2 cups flour
1 (8 ounce) sour cream

TOPPING:

1/2 cup chopped nuts
2 teaspoons sugar

2 teaspoons cinnamon

Cream first seven ingredients in large mixing bowl. Add sour cream and flour, alternatingly, mixing well after each addition. Combine topping ingredients in separate bowl. Pour half of the batter in a greased tube cake pan. Sprinkle half of the topping mixture over batter. Pour remaining batter in the pan and sprinkle remainder of the topping mixture on top. Bake at 350° for 55 minutes. Cool 1 1/2 hours before removing from the pan.

Mrs. David H. Sherwood (Virginia)
Bristol, Virginia

"May I ask you to bring up some herbs from the garden to make a savory omelet? Sage and thyme, and mint and two onions, and some parsley. I will provide lard for the stuff—lard for the omelet," said the hospitable gentleman with sandy whiskers.

Beatrix Potter

BREAKFAST BRUNCH CAKE

Oven: 350° 40 to 45 minutes   Yield: 1 cake

1 box Duncan Hines butter cake mix
1 small box (3 1/2 oz.) instant French vanilla pudding
3/4 cup corn oil (Crisco or Wesson)
3/4 cup water
4 large eggs
1 teaspoon vanilla flavoring
1 teaspoon butter flavoring
1 teaspoon almond flavoring
1 cup chopped pecans
1 stick butter or margarine
2 teaspoons ground cinnamon
1/4 cup granulated sugar

Take one whole stick of butter and use what you need of it to grease bottom and sides of bundt pan well. Flour lightly. Use remaining butter and cut into blobs, placing them around bottom of pan. Sprinkle pecans all around on top of this.

Mix together cake and pudding mix. Add oil and water. Mix well. Add one egg at a time and beat after each. Add the three flavorings. Beat at high speed for eight minutes.

Pour 1/3 of batter into pan; sprinkle with half of sugar and cinnamon mixture. Add another third of batter and sprinkle with remaining sugar and cinnamon. Add remaining batter. Bake at 350° 40 to 45 minutes. Cool 8 minutes in pan. Remove and drizzle with glaze while warm. Can be frozen.

Glaze

1 cup 10X powdered sugar
1/2 teaspoon clear vanilla flavoring (clear)
1/2 teaspoon butter flavoring
1/2 teaspoon almond flavoring
1 tablespoon milk

Mix ingredients.

Mrs. Harold Lawrence (Michelle)

BEER BREAD

Oven: 375° 40 minutes; then 20 minutes   Yield: 1 loaf

3 cups self-rising flour
3 tablespoons sugar
1 12 ounce can of beer

1 stick of butter or
  margarine, melted

Mix flour, sugar and beer together and pour into greased loaf pan. Pour 3/4 stick of melted butter on top. Bake for 40 minutes. Add remainder of butter over top and bake another 20 minutes. Allow 5 to 10 minutes to cool and turn out of loaf pan.

Mrs. Carolyn Connell
Hollonville, Georgia

DILLY BREAD

Oven: 350 degrees
30 to 35 minutes   Yield: 2 large or 3 small loaves

2 packages yeast
1/2 cup warm water
2 cups cottage cheese
2 tablespoons sugar
2 tablespoons minced onion
2 tablespoons real butter

4 teaspoons dill seed
2 teaspoons salt
1/2 teaspoon soda
2 unbeaten eggs
4 to 5 cups flour

Combine yeast and warm water. Combine next eight ingredients. Add yeast to cheese mixture. Add 4 to 5 cups flour to form a stiff dough, beating well after each addition of flour. Let rise in warm place until double in size (50 to 60 minutes). Stir down dough, adding more flour if needed to handle. Turn into greased loaf pan. Let rise 40 to 50 minutes. Brush with soft butter and sprinkle with salt. Bake at 350 degrees for 30 to 35 minutes. Makes 2 large or 3 small loaves.

Mrs. Lawrence W. Keith (Jane)

CHEESE BISCUITS
Great with strawberry preserves

Oven: 300° 20 minutes   Yield: 4 dozen

1 1/4 pounds cheddar cheese,   4 cups flour
   grated   1 scant teaspoon salt
3/4 pound butter, room   pinch of pepper (optional)
   temperature   1 teaspoon baking powder

Cream butter and cheese. Add flour, salt, pepper and baking powder. Make a firm dough and knead until smooth and rather stiff. (Use extra flour if necessary.) Roll very thin and cut with a small biscuit cutter (about 1 1/4 inches in diameter). Bake at 300° for approximately 20 minutes. Roll in powdered sugar while warm, if desired.

Mrs. Duke Blackburn (Julia)

CORNMEAL CRISPS

Oven: 350° 25 minutes   Yield: 4 to 6 servings

1 cup plain cornmeal   2 1/2 tablespoons
1 cup boiling water   butter/margarine
                                    1/2 teaspoon salt

Add cornmeal gradually to boiling water. When smooth, stir in butter and salt. Spread evenly on buttered baking sheet to 1/8 inch thickness. Bake at 350° about 25 minutes (or until well browned). Cut or break into squares. Serve at once.

Mrs. Robert Marchman, Jr. (Lois)
Fort Valley, Georgia

SPOON CORNBREAD

Oven: 350° 1 hour

2 eggs
1 8 1/2 oz. box Jiffy
  cornbread mix
1 can creamed corn
  (17 oz. size)

1 can whole kernel corn
  (17 oz. size)
1 stick butter, melted
1 cup sour cream

Mix all together. Bake in deep-dish greased iron skillet for 1 hour.

Mrs. Robert P. Campbell, Jr. (Fran)

HOT MEXICAN CORNBREAD

Oven: Preheat to 350°   Yield: 12 servings

1 box Ballard corn bread mix
2 cups buttermilk
2 cups Wesson oil
3 tablespoons flour
2 eggs

1 large can cream corn
3 large onions, chopped
12 pods hot pepper, chopped
2 or 3 pods bell pepper,
  chopped

Mix corn bread mix, buttermilk, oil and flour. Beat eggs into mixture thoroughly. Stir in remaining ingredients. Pour into 12x9 pan and bake until brown.

VARIATION: Add 1 cup grated cheese.

Mrs. L. Stephen Mitchell (Linda)

"A loaf of bread," the Walrus said, "Is what we chiefly need;
Pepper and vinegar besides—are very good indeed."

Lewis Carroll

HERB BUTTERS

Butter can be made days in advance and chilled or frozen. Using food processor or mixer, cream softened butter until light and fluffy. Blend in flavors, shape and chill. Shaped butter may be coated in parsley or paprika. Put flavored butters in crock or use one of the following methods of shaping butter:

1. Put in individual butter molds.
2. Shape like commercial stick of butter; chill until firm; roll in crushed herbs or confectioner's sugar and slice into squares, slice with fluted knife, or cut into curls using a butter curler.
3. Shape into balls and roll in crushed herbs or confectioner's sugar.
4. Spread into 1/2" thick layer, chill until firm and cut with a 1" canape cutter.
5. Chill until piping consistency and pipe 1" squiggles.

FRUIT BUTTER
Wonderful on biscuits, muffins, breads, waffles and pancakes

1 cup butter, softened
2 teaspoons lemon juice
1 cup confectioner's sugar
(more or less depending on
sweetness of fruit)

1 cup fresh or frozen fruit,
mashed (strawberries,
peaches, raspberries,
blueberries)

Using mixer or food processor, beat butter until light and fluffy. Beat in lemon juice and sugar. Beat in mashed fruit slowly (a spoonful at a time) until evenly absorbed.

HONEY BUTTER

1 cup butter, softened
1/4 cup honey

1 teaspoon cinnamon,
optional

Process butter in mixer or food processor. Add honey slowly. Add cinnamon, if desired.

MAPLE OR PECAN BUTTER

1 cup butter, softened   1/2 cup pecan or maple syrup

Process butter as above and add syrup slowly.

HERB BUTTERS
Use on grilled meats, steamed vegetables, baked potatoes or rolls

HERBED BUTTER

1/2 cup butter, softened
1 teaspoon chives
1/2 teaspoon dill

1/2 teaspoon chopped fresh
  parsley
3/4 teaspoon lemon juice
dash tabasco sauce

PEPPER BUTTER

1/2 cup butter, softened
1/2 teaspoon tabasco sauce

1 tablespoon minced sweet
  red pepper

PARSLEY BUTTER

1/2 cup butter, softened
1 tablespoon chopped fresh
  parsley
1/4 teaspoon salt

3/4 teaspoon chopped fresh
  basil
1 small clove garlic, minced

CHERVIL BUTTER

1/2 cup butter, softened
2 to 3 tablespoons minced
  fresh chervil (or 1/2 to 1

tablespoon dried whole
  chervil)

PAPRIKA BUTTER

1/2 cup butter, softened
1/2 teaspoon sugar
1/2 teaspoon tomato paste

Dash cayenne pepper
Paprika

GARLIC BUTTER

1/2 cup butter, softened
Dash salt

2 cloves garlic, minced

FRENCH TOAST

Yield: 2 servings

3 eggs
3/4 cup milk
1 tablespoon sugar
1/4 teaspoon salt

4 slices white bread 3/4"
thick
2 tablespoons butter
Confectioners' sugar

In a small bowl, with a rotary beater, beat eggs, milk, sugar, and salt until smooth and blended. In a 9" square baking dish, arrange the bread in a single layer. Pour egg mixture over bread; turn to coat evenly. Refrigerate covered overnight. In half of the butter in skillet, sauté bread until golden brown, about 4 minutes on a side. Add butter as needed. Dust lightly with confectioners' sugar.

Mrs. Charlie Adams (Jeanene)

ED DODD'S SOUR DOUGH FLAPJACKS

Yield: 4 to 6 servings

1 (1/4 ounce) package dry
yeast
1 cup warm water
1 1/4 cup flour (more or less
to taste)

1 egg
3/4 teaspoon salt
3 tablespoons sugar
1/4 teaspoon baking soda

Put yeast in a deep bowl, add warm water, and stir until dissolved. Add enough flour to make batter as stiff as waffle batter. Cover bowl and let stand overnight in a warm place. Next morning, add unbeaten egg, salt, sugar, and baking soda. Mix well and cook on a hot griddle.

(Thin out batter with warm water if flapjacks are too thick; add more flour if too thin.)

Mrs. Frank Bassett Jarrell (Marion)
Atlanta, Georgia

VILLAGE PANCAKES
Good served for brunch along with fresh strawberries and bacon

Yield: 4 servings

1 cup all-purpose flour
1/2 teaspoon salt
1 tablespoon sugar
1 cup sour cream

1 cup small-curd cottage
cheese
4 large eggs, beaten until
foamy

Stir together flour, salt and sugar. Add sour cream, cottage cheese and eggs and gently beat just until flour mixture is moistened. Drop by 1/4 cupfuls, well apart, onto a hot, oiled griddle. Cook until bubbles break, turn and brown other side. Serve with maple syrup.

Mrs. J.W. Owens (Elon)

SOUR CREAM COFFEE CAKE

Oven: Preheat to 350°

Yield: 1 cake

BATTER:
1 1/2 cups self-rising flour
3/4 cup sugar
1 cup sour cream (or 1/2 cup
  milk & 1/2 cup sour cream)

1 cup shortening
1 egg

TOPPING:
1/3 cup flour
1/4 cup butter

1/2 cup sugar
1 tablespoon cinnamon

GLAZE:
1 cup powdered sugar
1 tablespoon milk

1/2 teaspoon vanilla

Mix batter ingredients together until smooth. Pour into greased and floured bundt pan. Mix topping ingredients together and place on top of batter. Bake for 25 to 30 minutes. Mix glaze ingredients together and pour over hot cake.

Susan Todd

63

SCRAMBLED EGG CASSEROLE

Oven: 350° 30 minutes   Yield: 6 servings

1/2 cup cubed ham
2 tablespoons chopped onion
1 1/2 tablespoons melted
  butter
6 eggs, beaten
1 (1.4 ounce) can sliced
  mushrooms, drained

Cheese sauce (recipe below)
2 tablespoons melted butter
1 cup bread crumbs
Paprika

Sauté ham and onion in 1 1/2 tablespoons melted butter. Add eggs. Cook over medium heat until eggs are set, stirring to form large, soft curd. Stir in mushrooms and cheese. Spoon into greased Pyrex dish. Combine 2 tablespoons melted butter and bread crumbs. Spread over eggs. Sprinkle with paprika, cover and chill overnight. Uncover and bake at 350° for 30 minutes until heated.

CHEESE SAUCE:

1 tablespoon butter
1/4 tablespoon flour
1 cup milk
1/4 teaspoon salt

Dash pepper
1/2 cup shredded cheddar
  cheese

Melt butter in saucepan over low heat. Blend in flour and cook 1 minute. Gradually add milk and cook until thickened, stirring constantly. Add salt, pepper and cheese, stirring until smooth.

Mrs. Guilford Connally

"All that's sweet was made, but to be lost when sweetest."

Moore

BREAKFAST EGG PIZZA

Oven: 425° 20 minutes   Yield: 6 servings

1 package of 8 crescent rolls
8 ounces swiss cheese, grated
8 ounces sausage (patties)
3/4 cup milk
4 eggs

1 teaspooon salt
1/4 teaspoon pepper
1/4 teaspoon oregano
1/4 teaspoon thyme

Spread out rolls on 13"x9" pan and lap up on edges. Cover bottom with grated cheese. Put sausage on top of cheese. Blend milk, eggs, and spices in blender and pour over sausage and cheese. Cook for 20 minutes at 425°. Slice and serve.

Mrs. Tom Carson (Nancy)

MEXICAN EGG CASSEROLE

Oven: 350° 40 to 45 minutes   Serves: 10 to 12

10 eggs
1/2 cup flour (all purpose)
1/2 teaspoon baking powder
1/2 teaspoon salt
1 pint creamy small-curd
   cottage cheese

1/2 cup melted butter or
   margarine
2 small (4 oz.) cans diced
   green chili peppers
1 lb. Monterey Jack cheese,
   shredded

Preheat oven to 350°. Beat eggs about 5 minutes until fluffy. Beat in other ingredients except cheese and chilies. Stir in peppers. Pour into a greased 9x13" Pyrex dish. Sprinkle all of cheese on top. Bake at 350° for 40 to 45 minutes or until center is firm. Serve immediately.

Mrs. Ann Arnold

MRS. HUGH CAMP'S HAM & EGG PIE

Oven: 350° 25 minutes   Yield: 6 to 8 servings

2 cups or more cooked ham,
  cubed or thin sliced
2 to 3 cups ham broth (or hot
  water flavored with 2
  bouillon cubes)
4 eggs

Pepper to taste
1 teaspoon worcestershire
  sauce
Dash of hot sauce
Pastry (or biscuits)

Line casserole or deep cake pan with pastry (or biscuits rolled thin). Put ham in casserole with enough broth to cover generously. Add each egg, unbeaten, separately spaced from other eggs. Add seasonings. Place rolled pastry or uncooked biscuits on top. Bake at 350° for 25 minutes.

Miriam C. Miller
Moreland, Georgia

HAM QUICHE

Oven: 350° 45 to 50 minutes   Yield: 6 servings

1 pie pastry, baked
1/2 cup mayonnaise
2 tablespoons all purpose
  flour
4 eggs, beaten

1/2 cup milk
1 cup diced fully cooked ham
1 cup shredded cheddar
  cheese
1 cup shredded Swiss cheese

Combine mayonnaise, flour, eggs and milk. Mix thoroughly. Stir in ham and cheese and pour into baked pie shell. Bake at 350° for 45 to 50 minutes.

Mrs. Joe Distel (Pat)

BEDEVILED BACON

Oven: 350° about 35 minutes

Thick sliced bacon
1 egg
1/2 teaspoon dry mustard

1/2 teaspoon cayenne pepper
1 teaspoon vinegar
Crushed cracker crumbs

Preheat oven to 350°. Cut thick sliced bacon in halves. Beat the egg with a fork and add dry mustard, cayenne pepper and vinegar. Dip bacon in egg mixture, then in finely crushed cracker crumbs. Place on rack and bake in oven preheated to 350° until crisp and brown (About 35 minutes).

Mrs. Scott Arrowsmith (Sandey)

VENISON (OR PORK) SAUSAGE LOAF

Oven: 350° 1 hour   Yield: 4 servings

1 lb. venison sausage (works
    well w/pork sausage too)
3/4 cup oatmeal (quick or
    regular)
1 large apple
1/2 teaspoon salt
3/4 teaspoon basil

3/4 teaspoon sage
1 egg
2/3 cup milk
1 (16 ounce) can
    unsweetened peaches,
    slices or halves

Preheat oven to 350°. Mix all ingredients except peaches. Line a loaf pan with peaches (no need to grease pan). Press meat into pan on top of peaches. Bake at 350° for 1 hour. Invert pan over a rack and let stand until grease drains. Unmold and serve.

Mrs. Sam O. Candler (Betsy)
Sharpsburg, Georgia

SAUSAGE AND WILD RICE CASSEROLE

Oven: 350° 30 minutes   Yield: 8 to 10 servings

2 pounds sausage (hot or
  mild)
1 onion, chopped
1 can (4 ounce) water
  chestnuts

1 can (4 ounce) mushrooms
1 small box wild rice
2 cans cream of mushroom
  soup

Brown sausage, drain and save enough grease to sauté onions. Sauté onions, water chestnuts, and mushrooms. Add to sausage and set aside. Cook rice. Combine rice, sausage and mushroom soup. Pour in casserole dish and bake at 350° for 30 minutes. Top with cheese or toasted almonds.

ALTERATION: Instead of mushroom soup, you can make your own cream sauce.

1 can chicken broth   2 tablespoons margarine
1/4 cup flour

Melt margarine in pan, add flour and brown. Add chicken broth to make cream sauce.

Mrs. Harry Hunter (Margaret)

BROILED BREAKFAST SANDWICHES

Broil: 2 to 3 minutes   Yield: 6 servings

1/2 (8 ounce) container
  whipped cream cheese
2 tablespoons milk
3 ounce package corned beef
  (chopped)

2 hard cooked eggs, chopped
1/2 cup shredded Swiss cheese
6 English muffin halves

Combine cream cheese and milk until smooth. Add beef, eggs, and Swiss cheese. Spread on English muffin halves and broil 2 to 3 minutes. Garnish with more hard cooked eggs, if desired.

Mrs. Stanley Lanier (Debbie)

CONDIMENTS

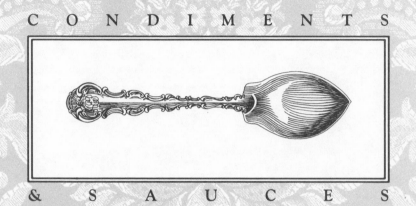

& SAUCES

Mayonnaise Server

CONDIMENTS

SAUCES

ELM STREET SCHOOL PIMENTO CHEESE

4 ounces pimento, chopped   1/2 cup mayonnaise
10 ounces sharp cheddar   Black pepper to taste
   cheese, grated

Mix together in food processor or with mixer. Store in refrigerator.

Mrs. Eugene Jackson (Ruth)
Elm Street School

"They dined upon mince and slices of quince, which they ate with a runcible spoon."

Edward Lear

PECAN BUTTER

1 cup butter or margarine   1/2 cup pecan syrup

Beat at high speed until fluffy. Serve on biscuits, pancakes, or favorite bread.

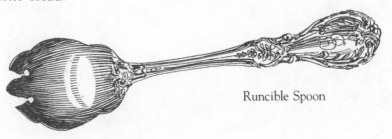

Runcible Spoon

LOW SODIUM SEASONING I

1 teaspoon chili powder
2 teaspoons oregano
2 teaspoons pepper
1 tablespoon garlic powder
2 tablespoons dry mustard

2 tablespoons poultry
  seasoning
6 tablespoons onion powder
3 tablespoons paprika

Mix and put in salt shaker.

Footed Salt Dish

LOW SODIUM SEASONING II

3 oz. powdered vegetable
  broth
1/4 teaspoon garlic powder
1/8 teaspoon powdered thyme
1/4 teaspoon onion powder

1/4 teaspoon paprika
1/8 teaspoon ground celery
  seed
1/4 teaspoon white pepper
1/4 teaspoon dry mustard

Mix and store in airtight jar.

ARTICHOKE RELISH

Yield: 12 pints

6 bell peppers, cut up
1 quart onions, chopped
3 pounds white cabbage,
  chopped
2 cups salt (for soaking)
1 gallon water
1 (24 ounce) jar prepared
  yellow mustard
3/4 cup flour

3 pounds sugar
1 tablespoon turmeric
1 tablespoon black pepper
1 tablespoon mustard seed
1/2 gallon vinegar
3 quarts (5 pounds)
  Jerusalem artichokes,
  scrubbed and coarsely
  chopped

Soak peppers, onions and cabbage in salt and water overnight. Next morning, strain vegetables. Make a paste of mustard, flour, sugar, turmeric, black pepper and mustard seed. Add vinegar and let cook 10 minutes. Add cabbage mixture and cook 8 more minutes. Add artichokes and cook 2 to 3 minutes, just long enough to heat through. Put in sterilized jars.

Mr. and Mrs. William M. Berry, Jr. (Jane)

POMANDER BALLS

Stick cloves in orange (or apple), barely touching, until all the fruit is covered. Let dry. Hang in closets, pile on evergreens with Christmas balls. Fasten on wooden sticks and insert in dried flower arrangements. Put among sheets and other household linens.

LAKE BURTON PICKLED EGGS

1 cup tarragon vinegar
1 cup water
1/2 teaspoon celery seed
2 tablespoons sugar

1 teaspoon salt
1 clove garlic
2 bay leaves
12 hard boiled eggs (peeled)

Simmer above mixture for 30 minutes. Pour over hard boiled eggs. Cover and refrigerate for 2 or 3 days.

Mrs. William M. Berry, III (Anne Jarrell)

 ## CITRUS RELISH
Good served with chicken, pork, or at brunch with sausage

Yield: 3 cups

2 apples, cored but not peeled
1 grapefruit
1 orange

1 tablespoon lime juice
1 cup sugar

Chop apples in food processor. Peel grapefruit, remove all membrane and seeds. Cut in small pieces. Quarter the orange, remove seeds and process in food processor. Combine all ingredients and chill overnight to blend flavors.

Mrs. Frank Marchman (Beth Candler)

"No spectacle on earth is more appealing than a beautiful woman . . . cooking dinner for someone she loves."

Thomas Wolfe

CURRIED MAYONNAISE

Yield: Serves 50 as a dip

2 cups Hellmann's
  mayonnaise
1 teaspoon lemon juice
2 teaspoons tarragon vinegar

2 teaspoons grated onion
1 or 2 teaspoons horseradish
1 teaspoon curry powder

Mix all ingredients at least two days ahead to let season. Additional 1/2 teaspoon curry powder may be needed. Recipe may be doubled. Keeps for weeks in refrigerator.

Can be used as dip for raw vegetables or spread for meat sandwiches. Good on fresh asparagus with sliced or grated hard boiled egg on lettuce salad.

Mrs. Minerva Cole Woodruff

"Condiments are like old friends, highly thought of, but often taken for granted."

Marilyn Kayton

CURRY POWDER

Equal parts ground:
  Tumeric
  Coriander
  Cumin

Ginger
Nutmeg
Mace
Cayenne pepper

FLAVORED VINEGAR

Garlic Flavor:

8 ounces distilled white vinegar   **1 clove garlic**

Insert wooden skewer into garlic clove. Place in a sterilized jar and fill with vinegar. Let stand for two weeks.

Lemon Flavor:

1 quart white vinegar   **Rind of 4 lemons cut in strips (use only zest of rind)**

Heat vinegar and lemon rind to boiling. Boil for one minute and pour into sterilized jar. Cool. Cover and let stand for two weeks at room temperature. Strain and discard lemon rind.

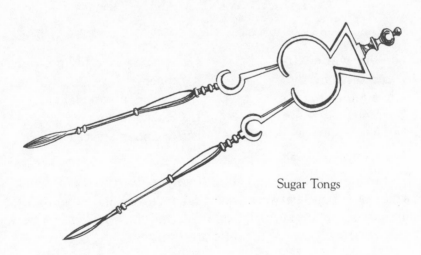

Sugar Tongs

BASIC BASTING SAUCE

Yield: 1 quart

1/4 cup olive or salad oil
3/4 cup chopped onion
1 clove garlic chopped
1 cup honey
1 cup catsup
1 cup wine vinegar

1/2 cup worcestershire sauce
1 tablespoon dry mustard
1 1/2 teaspoon salt
1 teaspoon oregano
1 teaspoon black pepper
1/2 teaspoon thyme

Heat salad or olive oil in saucepan. Add onion and garlic. Cook until tender. Add other ingredients. Cook to a boil stirring constantly. Cook another 5 minutes this time very slowly. This all purpose sauce can be poured into sterile jars, sealed and stored. Makes 1 quart. Perfect for basting hamburgers, spareribs, chicken, chops, etc.

Mrs. Lawrence W. Keith (Jane)

ITALIAN WINE MARINADE

Yield: 2 cups

1 cup dry white wine
1/2 cup olive oil
1 clove minced garlic
1/2 cup grated onion
1 teaspoon salt
2 tablespoons vinegar

1/2 teaspoon freshly ground
  pepper
1/2 teaspoon rosemary
1/2 teaspoon thyme
1/2 teaspoon sweet basil

Mix all ingredients and partially pulverize the rosemary, thyme, and basil between your index finger and thumb when adding. Use as an overnight marinade for chicken, lamb or pork. Brush meat with marinade while grilling.

John Ehrenhard

TURKISH YOGURT MARINADE

Yield: 3 cups

2 cups unflavored yogurt
1 cup grated onions
2 teaspoons salt

1 teaspoon fresh ground
pepper

Mix all ingredients and use as an overnight marinade for lamb.

John Ehrenhard

AFRICAN SAUCE FOR GRILLED STEAK

3 tablespoons olive oil
1 cup chopped green onions
1/2 cup chopped bell pepper
1 cup chopped fresh tomatoes
1 1/2 teaspoons salt

1 teaspoon Louisiana hot
sauce
1 teaspoon paprika
1 cup of finely ground
peanuts
1 1/2 cups beef broth
1/4 cup heavy cream

Heat oil in skillet and sauté onions and peppers 5 minutes. Add tomatoes, salt, hot sauce and paprika; cook over low heat for another 5 minutes and then mix in peanuts and broth; cook 30 minutes, stirring occasionally. Stir in cream and taste for seasoning. Serve with a grilled flank steak.

John Ehrenhard

CHICKEN MARINADE

1/2 cup soy sauce
1/2 cup oil
1/4 cup water
1/4 cup honey

1 tablespoon curry powder
1 teaspoon garlic salt
1 teaspoon pepper
1 tablespoon onion flakes

Marinade chicken overnight. Cook on grill.

Mrs. Peter Gaillard (Cheryl)

KENSINGTON MARINADE
for chicken or shrimp

Yield: 1 gallon

1 pint soy sauce
1 pint straight California
Sherry
1 1/4 cans (46 ounce)
pineapple juice

1/2 pint red wine vinegar
1 1/2 cups sugar
2 tablespoons Accent
1 scant tablespoon granulated
garlic

Marinate 24-48 hours.

Mrs David Cotton (Pat)

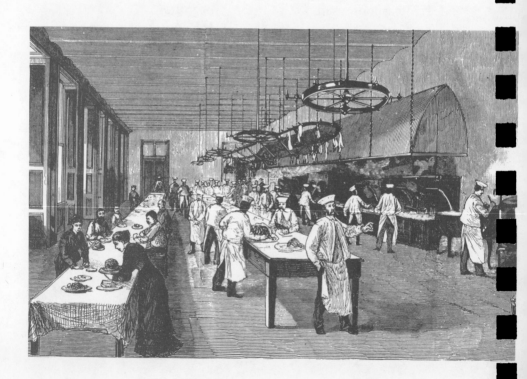

PEPPER SHERRY SAUCE

An African recipe; delicious served with bean soup, ham bone soup or vegetable soup. Also makes an unusual gift; give it with a bag of bean soup mix.

750 ml bottle Golden sherry
Fresh cayenne peppers
Dry whole ginger root (size
  of thumb)

1 teaspoon whole mixed
  pickling spice
1/8 teaspoon Tabasco sauce
1 tablespoon Worcestershire
  sauce

Fill a liter bottle 1/3 full of peppers. Add dry ginger root, spices, and sherry. Age for two weeks. (If it is too hot for your taste, add more sherry).

Mrs. Frank B. Jarrell (Marion)

JEZEBEL SAUCE

1 (6 ounce) jar Dijon
  mustard
1 (6 ounce) jar horseradish

1 (8 to 10 ounce) jar apple
  jelly
1 (8 or 10 ounce) jar
  pineapple preserves

Combine ingredients. Serve as sauce with ham or egg roll or pour over cream cheese and serve with crackers.

Mrs. William M. Berry, Junior (Jane)

COCKTAIL SAUCE

1 cup chili sauce
1/2 cup tomato catsup
1 tablespoon tarragon vinegar
1 teaspoon worcestershire
  sauce

1 teaspoon grated horseradish
Juice of 1 lemon
1/4 teaspoon celery salt
6 drops of Tabasco sauce

Mix together thoroughly.

Mrs. Lawrence W. Keith, Jr. (Jane)

ELM STREET SCHOOL'S BARBEQUE SAUCE
For a Crowd

Yield: 5 gallons

3 gallons vinegar
2 gallons ketchup
1 quart worcestershire sauce
1 tablespoon red pepper
2 tablespoons black pepper

2 tablespoons salt
2 pounds sugar
2 lemons, cut in half
2 onions, cut in half

Mix all ingredients, reserving 1 gallon of ketchup, and bring to a boil. Reduce heat. Add remaining gallon of ketchup and simmer for 30 minutes. Remove lemons and onions and serve over chopped pork or turkey.

Mrs. Eugene Jackson (Ruth)
Elm Street School

BARBECUE SAUCE

1 cup catsup
1 cup water
1 teaspoon chili powder
1/4 cup brown sugar

1/4 cup vinegar
1/4 cup worcestershire sauce
1/2 teaspoon mixed herb
   seasoning

Mix all the ingredients and bring to a boil. Add sauce to pork chops, chicken, spareribs, etc.

Mrs. Larry Strickland (Montie)

Steaming is one of the smartest ways to cook vegetables because the cooking liquid never touches the food. Most vegetables will steam in 10 minutes or less.

MICROWAVE MUSHROOM TOPPING

Microwave: high for 5 minutes
(repeat process 3 more times)

Yield: 8 servings

2 pounds of fresh mushrooms
  (firm and white)
1/4 stick of butter

1/4 to 1/2 cup soy sauce
  (your taste determines)

Rinse mushrooms and cut off 1/4 inch of the stem. Place all of the ingredients in a 2 or 2 1/2 quart casserole dish, (microwave safe). Cover with lid and cook on high for 5 minutes. Remove lid and stir. Repeat process 3 more times.

Great accompaniment for beef dishes, steak or tenderloin. Can prepare the day before or early in the day, refrigerate and reheat when ready to use.

Mrs. Charles M. Smith (Lynn)

MICROWAVE WHITE SAUCE

2 tablespoons butter
2 tablespoons flour
1/4 teaspoon salt

1/8 teaspoon pepper
1/4 teaspoon dry mustard
1 cup milk

Melt butter in quart size measuring cup on high for 30 seconds. Add flour and seasonings; stir well. Add a little of the milk and stir until smooth, then add the rest of the milk and stir well. Microwave for 2 minutes on high. Stir well and microwave for 2 minutes, until sauce thickens.

Bad dinners go hand in hand with total depravity; while a properly fed man is already half saved.

The Dixie Cook-Book (1888)

HOLLANDAISE SAUCE

2 egg yolks
1/2 lemon (juice only) fresh

1 stick butter or margarine
(cut into 8 pieces)

Put egg yolks in small sauce pan. Add lemon juice. Stir with wooden spoon. Stir constantly on lowest setting on burner. Add one piece of butter at a time to egg yolk mixture, stirring until melted. Stir until sauce is medium thick. Be patient!

Mrs. Robert Teller (Nancy)

MICROWAVE HOLLANDAISE SAUCE

Microwave: high for 20 seconds,
high for 1 minute

Yield: 4 servings
(1 cup)

1 stick butter or margarine
3 large egg yolks

Juice from 1/2 fresh lemon
(about 1 1/2 tablespoons)

Put butter in 4 cup measure. Microwave on high 20 seconds to soften, but not melt, (cold butter may need up to a minute). Mix egg yolks and lemon juice. Add to butter. Microwave on high about 1 minute, whipping with a wisk every 15 seconds. Makes 1 cup. The butter may be lumpy after the first two whippings, but will smooth out. When the sauce is smooth and thick, it is done; further cooking will cause the sauce to separate or curdle.

Mrs. Jett Fisher (Carol)

Curdle Cure: *Put 2 tablespoons (1 ounce) milk in glass measure. Microwave on high 30 seconds to boil. Slowly whisk into curdled sauce until sauce becomes smooth.*

S O U P S

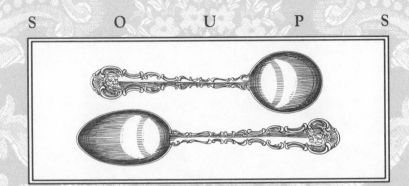

Clear & Cream Soup Spoons

SOUPS

CREAM VICHYSSOISE

Yield: 1 quart (4 servings)

2 large carrots, chopped fine
4 onions, chopped fine
2 potatoes, chopped fine
1 tablespoon butter
2 tablespoons olive oil (or
   butter may be substituted)
2 cups chicken stock

1 tablespoon uncooked rice
Salt to taste
Red pepper to taste
1 cup heavy cream (or milk)
Chopped parsley
Parmesan cheese (optional)

Cook carrots, onions and potatoes in butter and olive oil until very soft (about 10 minutes), stirring constantly. Add chicken stock and rice and simmer for 1 1/2 hours. Cool and add cream and reheat slowly, being careful not to boil. Top with chopped parsley and Parmesan cheese, if desired. (Note: Soup, minus the cream, may be frozen to be used later.)

Mrs. Cliff Glover (Inez)

CARROT CHOWDER

Yield: 6 servings

1 pound ground beef
1/2 teaspoon salt
1/2 cup diced celery
1/2 cup diced green pepper
1/2 cup chopped onion
4 cups tomato juice
2 cans cream of celery soup

1 1/2 cups water
2 large cloves garlic, minced
   (or 1/2 teaspoon garlic salt)
1/2 teaspoon pepper
1/2 teaspoon marjoram
2 1/2 cups shredded carrots
Sliced Swiss cheese

Brown ground beef with salt, celery, green pepper and onion. Set aside. In large saucepan, combine remaining ingredients, except Swiss cheese slices. Bring to boil. Add ground beef mixture and simmer for 45 minutes. Serve over Swiss cheese slices.

Mrs. Roddie Clifton (Connie)

MIRACLE SOUP
Burns calories and fat

Yield: 6 servings

2 carrots
6 to 8 onions
1 cabbage
1 stalk celery, including
   leaves

2 bell peppers
1 large can tomatoes
1 Lipton onion soup mix
beef or chicken bouillon for
   flavor (optional)

Cut up first 5 ingredients into bite-sized pieces. Cover with water and bring to boil for five minutes. Add tomatoes and onion soup and cook until desired tenderness (approximately 1 hour).

Mrs. David Cotton (Pat)

CHEESY BROCCOLI SOUP

Yield: 8 servings

HAM STOCK:

Hambone with some ham
attached
2 quarts water

1 tablespoon of cloves

SOUP:

2 lbs. of fresh broccoli or 1
small package of frozen
broccoli
1 onion (chopped)
3 carrots (grated)
4 cups of ham stock
5 cups milk

1 teaspoon salt
1/2 teaspoon pepper
8 oz. shredded swiss cheese
8 oz. shredded cheddar cheese
1/2 cup flour
2 cups ham, chopped
1/2 stick margarine

HAM STOCK:

Simmer bone in water with the cloves for about an hour in a covered pot. Remove from heat. Remove meat from the bone. Strain stock. Refrigerate. Skim off fat.

SOUP:

Wash broccoli and remove leaves and coarse stems. Chop broccoli coarsely. Boil first 3 ingredients in 1 1/2 cups of stock until tender. In a dutch oven or large boiler, add remaining stock, milk, salt, and pepper. Bring to a boil. Thoroughly coat cheese with the flour. Add cheese and flour gradually to milk and stock, stirring constantly. Cook at low heat until cheese is melted. Add vegetable mixture, ham and margarine. Heat to serving temperature.

Mrs. Robin Miller (Alice)

BROCCOLI SOUP

Yield: 5 cups

2 tablespoons grated onion
1/2 cup butter, melted
1/4 cup flour
1 cup milk
1 cup half and half

2 cups chicken broth
1/2 teaspoon salt
1/8 teaspoon garlic powder
1/4 to 1/2 teaspoon basil
3 cups chopped fresh broccoli

Sauté onion in butter. Add flour, stirring until smooth. Cook one minute, stirring constantly. Gradually add milk, half and half, and broth. Cook over medium heat, stirring constantly, until thick and bubbly. Stir in salt, garlic powder and basil. Add broccoli. Cover and cook on medium heat for 15 minutes. Be sure not to let milk boil. Blend soup mixture in blender and reheat to serve.

Mrs. O. Bryant Hunter (Victoria)

ELEGANT MUSHROOM SOUP

Yield: 4 cups

3/4 cup chopped green onions
2 cups chopped fresh
  mushrooms
1/4 cup butter or margarine,
  melted

2 tablespoons all-purpose
  flour
2 teaspoons chicken bouillon
  granules
2 cups boiling water
1 cup milk

Sauté onions and mushrooms in butter in a dutch oven until onions are tender. Stir in flour. Dissolve bouillon granules in boiling water. Gradually add bouillon mixture and milk to mushroom mixture. Cook over low heat 10 minutes or just until thoroughly heated.

Mrs. Thomas W. Morningstar (Donna)
Sharpsburg, Georgia

SPINACH SOUP

Yield: 4 to 6 servings

2 packages frozen spinach
2 tablespoons butter
1 onion, sliced
2 tablespoons flour

1 cup heavy cream
2 cups milk
1 chicken bouillon cube
1 cup hot water

Cook spinach as directed on package. Drain and squeeze out all water. Put through a food processor for best results. Melt butter and sauté onions. Stir in flour. Stir in milk and cream gradually. Melt bouillon cube in hot water and add to soup. Remove onion rings and discard. Heat through and serve. (It may be best to only sauté large onion rings, because it is hard to get all of the little pieces of onion out of the soup when finished.)

Carolyn C. Kee
Atlanta, Georgia

CRAB SOUP
A Tidewater Favorite

Yield: 6 servings

1/2 stick butter
1 tablespoon onion, chopped
6 tablespoons flour
1 teaspoon salt
1/2 teaspoon red pepper
1 teaspoon chopped parsley
1/8 teaspoon mace

1/8 teaspoon nutmeg
2 cups milk
1 pound crabmeat
2 cups half and half
8 tablespoons sherry or white
  wine

Sauté onion in butter. Add flour and next five ingredients. After heating, add milk and stir until thickened. Add crabmeat and simmer. In separate saucepan, heat half and half and sherry or white wine. When blended and warm, slowly blend into milk and crab mixture. Heat thoroughly, but DO NOT BOIL.

Brenda Murphey
Virginia Beach, VA

HOGAN'S HEROS' BACON & BLEU CHEESE SOUP

Yield: 12 servings

1 cup minced onions
1 cup bacon, cut into bit-sized
  pieces
2 bay leaves
8 cups chicken stock
2 pounds Bleu cheese
2 cups heavy cream

1 cup sour cream
2 tablespoons chopped parsley
2 tablespoons chopped chives
Salt to taste
Pepper to taste
Cayenne pepper to taste

Sauté onions and bacon until bacon is slightly crisp. Add bay leaves and chicken stock and boil for 20 minutes. Thicken with flour and cook 10 minutes more. Add Bleu cheese and stir in remaining ingredients.

Jeff Spader
Bubba Geer
Hogan's Heros
Hogansville, Georgia

BEER CHEESE SOUP
Originated from the Coburg Inn in New England

Yield: 8 servings

3/4 cup butter
1/2 cup diced celery
1/2 cup diced carrots
1/2 cup diced onion
1/2 cup flour
1/2 teaspoon dry mustard
1/4 teaspoon Accent

2 1/2 pints chicken stock
6 ounces grated cheddar
  cheese
2 tablespoons Parmesan
  cheese
1 (12 ounce) bottle of beer
Salt and pepper to taste

Sauté vegetables in butter until done. Blend in flour, mustard, Accent and chicken stock. Cook for 5 minutes. Blend in cheddar cheese, parmesan cheese and beer. Simmer for 30 minutes or until done.

Mrs. Keith Stewart (Anita)

FRENCH ONION SOUP (MICROWAVE)

Yield: 4 servings

3 tablespoons butter
1 pound sliced onions
6 cups warm water
4 beef bouillon cubes
1/2 teaspoon salt

Dash of pepper
1 cup shredded cheese (any
  kind, mozzarella is
  traditional)
4 toasted rounds of bread

Melt butter in 3 quart glass bowl on 100% power for 30 to 45 seconds. Add onions and cook covered on 100% power 10 to 12 minutes. Stir well. Measure water and dissolve bouillon cubes in it. Pour over onions. Cook on 100% power for 8 to 10 minutes. Add salt and pepper. Pour into 4 soup bowls. Place toast and cheese in bowls. Reheat in oven to melt cheese.

Mrs. Larry Deason (Sharon)

HAM BONE SOUP

Yield: 6 to 8 servings

1 Ham bone, after bone has
  been sliced
1 small onion
1 large can tomatoes
1 package frozen mixed
  vegetables (or 1 can Veg-all
  vegetables)

1 can whole kernel corn
3 carrots, cut into slices
2 cups vegetables, fresh,
  frozen or canned as lima
  beans, green beans, peas

Cook ham bone and onion in water to cover (about 2 quarts) until meat is tender. Remove meat from bone, return chopped meat to broth. Discard bone. Add remaining ingredients, simmer slowly until tender and flavors are mingled, about 20 minutes. Serve hot with cornbread.

Mrs. Ferrell Parrott (Emily)

BEAN SOUP MIX
Great gift idea; try layering beans in a wine bottle

Yield: 2 cups

1/3 cup dry baby lima beans
1/3 cup dry navy beans
1/3 cup dry blackeye peas
1/3 cup dry field peas
1/3 cup dry pinto beans

2 tablespoons dry green split peas
2 tablespoons dry lentils
2 tablespoons pearl barley

Combine all ingredients and store in zip lock bag.

BEAN SOUP

Yield: 8 servings

2 cups bean soup mix
2 tablespoons salt (soaking)
1 cup chopped ham (or ham hock)
2 quarts water
1 large onion
1 (28 ounce) can tomatoes
2 carrots, sliced

2 celery ribs, chopped
1/2 teaspoon dried basil
1/2 teaspoon oregano
1 bay leaf
Salt to taste
Pepper to taste
1/2 teaspoon cilantro (optional)

Wash beans thoroughly. Place in large pot and cover with water, add salt, and soak overnight. Next day, drain beans. Add 2 quarts water and ham or ham hock. Bring to a boil and simmer slowly 2 1/2 to 3 hours. Add remaining ingredients and simmer another 30 minutes. Garnish with rice, chopped onion, croutons, or pepper sherry.

Mrs. William M. Berry, III (Anne Jarrell)

TEXAS CHILI
Freezes well

Yield: 8 servings

4 pounds lean ground beef
1 large onion, chopped
2 cloves garlic, minced
1 bell pepper, chopped
  (optional)
1 teaspoon cumin seed
6 teaspoons chili powder
1 teaspoon oregano

6 dashes Tabasco sauce
1 teaspoon cayenne pepper
2 cups hot water
2 cups whole tomatoes
1 small can tomato sauce
Salt to taste
black pepper to taste
2 cans chili beans (optional)

Brown ground beef and drain off grease. Add onion, garlic (and bell pepper, if desired). Cook until transparent. Add other ingredients (use liquid in can of tomatoes to count for part of water) and simmer at least 1 1/2 hours. If grease rises, skim off before serving.

Mrs. L. Stephen Mitchell (Linda)

CHILI

Yield: 6 to 8 servings

1 to 1 1/2 pounds lean
  ground beef
1 large onion, chopped
2 cans chili or red kidney
  beans
1 to 2 (16 ounce) cans whole
  stewed tomatoes (depending
  on meat amount)

Chili powder to taste
1 tablespoon lemon juice
1 tablespoon worcestershire
  sauce
1/8 to 1/4 cup brown sugar
1 bay leaf

Brown ground beef and onions. Drain. Add other ingredients and simmer until thick.

Serve over rice with French bread and a salad, or serve with hotdogs and bread slices.

Mrs. N. Marshall Cawthon (Kay)

95

FIVE HOUR STEW

Oven: 250° 5 hours   Yield: 6 servings

2 pounds stew beef
4 carrots, quartered
2 potatoes, cut in chunks
1 onion, chopped
1 green pepper, cut in chunks

3 tablespoons minute tapioca
1 1/2 teaspoons salt
1 tablespoon sugar
1 (12 ounce) can vegetable
  cocktail juice

Place first five ingredients in a dutch oven. Sprinkle tapioca, salt and sugar over this. Pour the vegetable cocktail juice over all. Place tin foil, then lid tightly over this. Cook at 250° for 5 hours. No peeking!

Mrs. Larry Strickland (Montie)

HAMBURGER STEW

Yield: 4 to 6 servings

1 pound ground beef
1 medium onion, sliced
1 1/2 teaspoons salt
1/4 teaspoon pepper
1 tablespoon worcestershire
  sauce

1 (16 ounce) can tomatoes
3 medium potatoes, peeled
  and sliced
3 medium carrots, sliced
2 ribs celery, chopped

Brown ground beef and onions and drain. Add remaining ingredients and bring to boil. Simmer, covered, about 30 minutes or until vegetables are tender. Serve with corn bread, rice, or toast.

Jane Chambless
Sharpsburg, GA

Cajun Chili:
    Substitute black beans for kidney beans in your favorite chili recipe.

CHICKENNY BRUNSWICK STEW

Yield: 6 to 8 servings

2 1/2 to 3 pounds of chicken
2 stalks celery
1 small onion
2 quarts tomatoes (canned or fresh)
1 (10 1/2 ounce) can of butterbeans

1 (20 ounce) can corn (or 2 (8 ounce) cans of creamed)
3 medium potatoes, thinly cut
1 cup chopped onion (sautéed)
5 tablespoons sugar
1 tablespoon salt
1 teaspoon black pepper

Place chicken, celery, and onion in boiler and cook until tender. Remove chicken from bones and discard onion and celery. Allow liquid to cool and skim off fat. Return chicken to pot and add tomatoes, butterbeans, corn, potatoes, and onion. Add sugar, salt and pepper.

Simmer 2 hours, stirring often because this will burn easily. If using fresh vegetables, add them one at a time and cook some. Freezes well.

Mrs. Glen Connally (Sandy)

Beautiful Soup, so rich and green,
Waiting in a hot tureen!
Who for such dainties would not stoop?
Soup of the evening, beautiful soup!

Lewis Carroll

BEEF AND BARLEY VEGETABLE SOUP

Yield: 6-8 servings

1 pound ground chuck,
  cooked and drained
5 cups water
1 (14 1/2 ounce) can stewed
  tomatoes
1 (6 ounce) can V8 juice
1/2 cup barley
1/2 cup dried green split peas
1/2 cup chopped onion

1 tablespoon beef bouillon
1/4 teaspoon dried basil
1/2 teaspoon creole seasoning
1/4 teaspoon oregano
1/4 teaspoon pepper
1 bay leaf
3/4 cup chopped celery
3/4 cup sliced carrots

Combine first 13 ingredients in a large pot. Simmer 30 minute. Add carrots and celery and simmer 30 more minutes.

Mrs. William M. Berry, III (Anne Jarrell)

One morning in the garden bed, the onion and the carrot
  said, Unto the parsley group:
"Oh, when shall we three meet again?
In thunder, lightning, hail or rain?"
"Alas, replied in tones of pain,
The parsley, "In the soup."

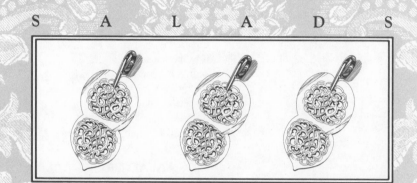

Congealed Salad Server

SALADS

FROZEN FRUIT SALAD

Yield: 9 servings

1 large can crushed pineapple
1 (21-ounce) can peach pie
  filling
1 (21-ounce) can strawberry
  pie filling

1 cup whipping cream,
  whipped
1 mashed banana (optional)
Mayonnaise
Lettuce

Mix all ingredients together and pour into 9x9 inch square pan. Freeze several hours. Cut into squares. Top each square with 1/2 teaspoon of mayonnaise and serve on lettuce leaf.

Mrs. Robin Miller (Alice)

FROZEN FRUIT SALAD

This recipe is easily doubled and can be frozen for 1 to 2 months

Yield: 6 servings

1 pint dairy sour cream
2 tablespoons lemon juice
3/4 cup sugar
1 (9 ounce) can of crushed
  pineapple, well drained

1/4 cup pecans, coarsely
  chopped
1/4 cup chopped cherries
1 banana, sliced

Mix first 4 ingredients; add remaining ingredients. Freeze in covered refrigerator dish or individual jello molds (I use jello molds). When frozen, turn them out and wrap individually and drop into a heavy freezer bag. They are ready to use any time.

Serve on a lettuce leaf.

Mrs. Cliff Glover (Inez)

Strawberry Fork

MANDARIN ORANGE SALAD

Yield: 8 servings

2 cups cottage cheese
1 (3-ounce) orange gelatin

1 can Mandarin oranges,
  drained
2 cups Cool Whip

Mix cottage cheese and gelatin. Stir in oranges. Fold in Cool Whip. Refrigerate until served.

Mrs. Larry Strickland (Montie)

COOL WHIP SALAD
Can also be used as a dessert

Yield: 4 to 6 servings

2 small cans Mandarin
  oranges
2 large cans dark sweet pitted
  cherries
1 large can chunk pineapple

1 (9-ounce) Cool Whip
1 can Eagle Brand condensed
  milk
1/4 cup real lemon juice

Drain oranges, cherries, pineapple and add to Cool Whip, Eagle Brand milk and lemon juice. Stir and refrigerate.

Mrs. Larry Deason (Sharon)

Let the stoics say what they please, we do not eat for the good for living, but because the meat is savory and the appetite is keen.

He that eats till he is sick, must fast till he is well.

Thomas Fuller

BERRY DIFFERENT SPINACH SALAD

Yield: 8 servings

1 pound fresh spinach
1 cup avocado
1/2 cup strawberries

2 tablespoons minced chives
(or green onions)

Sesame Seed Dressing (made ahead of time):

1/2 to 3/4 cup sugar
1/2 cup wine vinegar
1 cup salad oil
1/4 cup sesame seeds, toasted
1/2 teaspoon salt
1/2 teaspoon paprika

1/4 teasoon dry mustard
1/4 teaspoon Tabasco
1/4 teaspoon Worcestershire
sauce
3/4 teaspoon minced onion

Clean and thoroughly dry spinach. Tear into pieces, removing spines. Cut avocado into chunks, slice strawberries thinly. Mix all ingredients together in bowl. Combine all dressing ingredients in a blender and blend thoroughly. If dressing separates before using, blend before serving over salad. (Dressing is also good with fruit salad.)

Mrs. Scott Arrowsmith (Sandey)

Different Coleslaw:
    Roasted sunflower seeds
    chopped dates
    honey (stirred into the mayonnaise)

SPINACH-APPLE SALAD
A colorful, delicious and healthy salad

Yield: 6 servings

1 pound fresh spinach, trimmed and washed
3 small apples, chopped and unpeeled
2/3 cup corn oil
1/4 cup wine vinegar
1 tablespoon soy sauce
1 teaspoon dry mustard
1 teaspoon sugar
1/2 teaspoon salt
2 teaspoons fresh lemon juice
2 dashes hot pepper sauce
Freshly ground pepper
1/4 cup toasted sunflower seeds

Toss spinach and apples. In a pint jar shake all other ingredients except sunflower seeds. Add dressing to spinach and apples to coat well. Add sunflower seeds.

Mrs. Wright Lipford (Faye)

MOM'S CRANBERRY SALAD

1 can whole cranberry sauce
1 small crushed pineapple
1 cup pecans (finely chopped)
1/2 orange grated (juice and rind)
6 ounce package cherry Jello
1 cup finely chopped apple

Dissolve Jello in 2 cups hot water. Add orange juice and rind, pineapple, cranberry, nuts and apple. Chill and serve.

In memory of: Mrs. Faye V. Watson
St. Petersburg, Florida
Mrs. David Cotton (Pat)

ORANGE SALAD

Yield: 6 servings

12 ounces Cool Whip
Small sour cream
3 ounce box orange Jello

Small can crushed pineapple, drained
Small can mandarin oranges, drained

Combine Cool Whip, sour cream, and (dry) orange jello—stir well. Fold drained fruit into mixture. Chill in covered container until firm. *Optional:* Save a few mandarin oranges to garnish top, if desired.

Mrs. Alicia Smith
Smith's Country Store
Thomas Crossroads

CHERRY SALAD

Yield: 8 to 10 servings

1/4 cup cold water
Rind & juice of 1 lemon
Rind & juice of 1 orange
1 (3 ounce) cherry Jello

1 package plain Knox gelatin
1/2 cup sugar
1 large can crushed pineapple
1 large can pie cherries

Heat water, lemon juice and orange juice and add Jello and Knox gelatin to dissolve. Add sugar and cool mixture to lukewarm. Add pineapple and cherries. Place in container in refrigerator to congeal. Serve on lettuce bed.

Edith Sewell

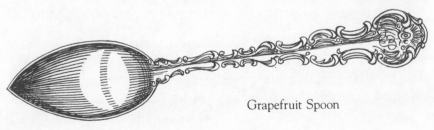

Grapefruit Spoon

CONGEALED VEGETABLE SALAD

Yield: 6 servings

2 (6 oz.) packages lemon
gelatin
1 1/2 cups boiling water
3 tablespoons sugar
1 tablespoon grated onion
1 teaspoon salt
1 tablespoon lemon juice
3/4 cup wine vinegar
1/2 cup finely grated carrots
1/2 cup finely chopped green
pepper

1 small jar pimento
1/2 cup pecans, finely
chopped
1/2 cup finely chopped celery
1 1/2 cups finely grated
cabbage
1 small can English peas,
drained
1/8 teaspoon ground red
pepper

Prepare gelatin with water and sugar. Add remaining ingredients and pour into Pyrex dish or mold. Prepare 1 or 2 days before you plan to serve it.

Mrs. Robert Cordle, Sr. (Verna)
West Point, Mississippi

ASHEVILLE SALAD
Pretty at Christmas

Yield: 12 servings

1 can tomato soup
2 (3 ounce) cream cheese
2 tablespoons plain gelatin
1/2 cup cold water
1 cup mayonnaise

1 cup chopped celery
1 tablespoon chopped bell
pepper
1 small chopped onion
1/4 to 1/2 cup chopped olives

Heat soup, undiluted, to boiling point. Add cream cheese and stir until smooth. Add gelatin which has been softened in cold water. When mixture is partially cooled, add mayonnaise and chopped vegetables. Chill in large mold.

Mrs. Jimmy Hutchinson (Jane)

WILLIASMBURG INN SALAD

Yield: 1 1/4 Quarts

2 envelopes unflavored gelatin
1/2 cup cold water
1 cup boiling water
1/2 cup vinegar
1/2 teaspoon salt
1/2 cup cold water
1 1/2 cup sugar

Few drops green food coloring
1 cup diced almonds
1 cup salad pickles (Delites)
1 cup crushed pinapple
  (drained)
1 cup sliced stuffed olives

Soften gelatin in 1/2 cup cold water, add to boiling water and stir until dissolved. Add 1/2 cup cold water, vinegar, salt, sugar and a few drops of green coloring. Stir until mixture thickens. Fold in other ingredients. Chill until ready to serve.

Mrs. Irwin H. Pike (Helen)

PRETZEL SALAD

Oven: 350° 10 minutes   Yield: 10 servings

2 cups boiling water
1 large strawberry jello
1 pound frozen strawberries
2 1/2 to 3 cups pretzels (small
  stick ones)
3/4 cup margarine, softened

3 tablespoons packed brown
  sugar
1 (8-ounce) cream cheese,
  softened
1 cup sugar
1 (9-ounce) Cool Whip

Dissolve jello in boiling water. Add strawberries and chill until thickened. Break up pretzels and put in colander. Shake to remove salt. Add margarine and mix with brown sugar. Press pretzel mixture in bottom of 9x13-inch dish and bake at 350° for 10 minutes. Allow to cool. Mix together cream cheese, sugar and Cool Whip and spread on top of "crust". Put strawberry mixture on top of cream cheese and refrigerate overnight.

Mrs. Robley Morrison (Ann)
Ashburn, Georgia

CONGEALED WALDORF SALAD

Yield: 6 servings

1 (3 ounce) package lemon
  gelatin
1 cup boiling water
2 tablespoons lemon juice
2 tablespoons sugar or sugar
  substitute

1 cup cold water
1/2 cup celery
3/4 cup slightly toasted
  pecans, chopped

Dissolve gelatin in hot water. Add lemon juice and sugar. Add cold water and stir. Refrigerate until partially congealed. Add nuts and celery and mix well. Chill until congealed.

Mrs. Carlton Ingram (Grace)

SEAFOOD VEGETABLE MOLD

May use canned salmon or crabmeat in place of tuna

Yield: 6 servings

1 envelope Knox Gelatin
1/4 cup cold water
1/4 cup hot water
2/3 cup mayonnaise
2 teaspoons prepared mustard
2 tablespoons lemon juice
1 (7 ounce) can tuna fish

3/4 cup minced celery
1/2 cup canned or cooked
  peas
2 tablespoons minced onion
2 tablespoons minced pimento
1 teaspoon salt
1 hard boiled egg, chopped

Soften gelatin in cold water and dissolve in hot water. In a separate bowl, combine mayonnaise, mustard and lemon juice. Add dissolved gelatin to mayonnaise. In separate bowl mix together remaining ingredients. Combine the two mixtures and pour into a loaf pan or mold that has been rinsed with cold water. Chill until firm. Unmold on lettuce leaves and garnish with olives and radish roses.

Mrs. J.T. Williams, Jr. (Willene)

CURRIED CHICKEN SALAD

Yield: 6 to 8 servings

1 head lettuce
1 package alfalfa sprouts
2 bunches green onions,
   chopped

2 cans water chestnuts, sliced
6 cups cooked chicken, cubed
2 large handful Chinese
   peapods

Topping

2 cups mayonnaise
1 tablespoon sugar

2 teaspoons curry
1/2 teaspoon ground ginger

Layer one day ahead; the lettuce in small pieces and the remainder of the ingredients. Spread on the topping. Refrigerate. Toss before serving. Top with cashews.

Mrs. Jett Fisher (Carol)

BOMBAY CHICKEN SALAD

Yield: 6 servings

2 cups cooked diced chicken
1 1/2 cups cold cooked rice
1 cup of chopped celery
1 tablespoon of lemon juice

1 teaspoon curry powder
Salt, pepper to taste
1/2 cup of mayonnaise

Condiments:

Chopped peanuts
Shredded coconut
Green seedless grapes

Chopped green peppers
Mandarin oranges
Mango or peach chutney

Combine chicken, rice and celery. Mix the rest of the ingredients and add to chicken mixture. Serve cold with a combination of condiments.

Mrs. Dennis McEntire (Sally)

CHUTNEYED TUNA CURRY SALAD

Yield: 4 servings

1/4 cup mayonnaise
1 (3-ounce) cream cheese, softened
1/4 cup heavy cream
1 to 1 1/2 teaspoons curry powder
1 1/2 teaspoons sugar
1 teaspoon grated lemon rind
1/2 teaspoon paprika
1 (11-ounce) can white solid tuna, drained
1/4 jar mango chutney
Lettuce

Blend mayonnaise and cream cheese together, add heavy cream. Mix in remainder of seasonings. Turn solid tuna out of can onto a bed of lettuce. Spoon sauce on top and put chutney on top of sauce.

Mrs. Jett Fisher (Carol)

PASTA SALAD

Yield: 8 servings

8 oz. spaghetti, cooked (small pieces) rinse in cold water
1 cup feta cheese, finely crumbled
4 medium tomatoes, chopped
1 cucumber, chopped
1 small green pepper, chopped
1 medium onion, chopped
1/4 cup fresh parsley, chopped

Dressing:

1/4 cup olive oil
1 tablespoon sugar
3 tablespoons white wine
2 tablespoons lemon juice
1/4 teaspoon white pepper
Dash of hot sauce

Mix ingredients well and pour over salad.
Mix all together preferably a day or two before serving so as to "mellow."

CHINESE SLAW

Serves: 12 to 15 people

1 can sliced water chestnuts
1 can mixed Chinese
  vegetables
1 can French style green
  beans
1 can sliced mushrooms

1 small jar diced pimiento
1 1/2 cup diced celery
1 (8 ounce) can peas
1 large onion, sliced in rings
3/4 cup wine vinegar
1 cup sugar

Drain all vegetables. Combine vinegar and sugar in sauce pan; bring to a boil. Pour over vegetables. Marinate over night. Salad will keep for 2 weeks in the refrigerator.

Mrs. Edwin L. Wyrick (Lois)
Sharpsburg, Georgia

CHINESE VEGETABLE SALAD
Good party dish

Yield: 8 servings

1 large can small English peas
1 large can seasoned beans
2 (#2) cans Chinese or chop
  suey vegetables with
  mushrooms
1 can sliced water chestnuts

1 small jar pimiento
1 large onion sliced thin
  (rings)
1 1/2 cups finely chopped
  celery

DRESSING:
3/4 cup apple cider vinegar
Salt to taste

1/2 cup sugar
Pepper to taste

Drain all vegetables well. Mix dressing ingredients and pour over combined vegetables. Let marinate for 24 hours.

Mrs. William Headley (Anita)

111

GREEN BEAN SALAD

Yield: 6 servings

3 cans whole Blue Lake green
beans
1 cup vinegar
1/4 cup bean juice

1 cup sugar
3/4 teaspoon salt
4 tablespoons oil
1/2 cup onions, chopped

Drain green beans reserving 1/4 cup of juice. Heat bean juice and vinegar to boiling point. Add sugar, salt, oil and onions. Pour over beans and chill.

Mrs. Frank Bassett Jarrell (Marion)
Atlanta, Georgia

BEAN SALAD

Yield: 8 servings

2 (#2) cans Blue Lake green
beans
1 can diced carrots
1/4 cup sugar
1/2 cup vinegar
1 3/4 cups oil
1 onion, sliced
2 stalks celery, chopped

1/2 bell pepper
1 (#2) can English peas
1/3 cup catsup
Juice of 1 lemon
1 teaspoon prepared mustard
1/2 teaspoon salt
Dash red pepper
Dash of garlic

Drain beans and carrots. Combine sugar, 1/4 cup vinegar and 3/4 cup oil well and pour over beans and carrots. Cover with onion slices and leave overnight. The next day, drain off marinade. Add celery, bell pepper and drained English peas. Combine 1 cup oil, catsup, 1/4 cup vinegar, lemon juice, mustard, salt, red pepper and garlic and beat until smooth. Pour over salad.

Mrs. Jimmy Hutchinson (Jane)

GREEN PEA SALAD

Yield: 10 servings

2 cups chopped celery
1 bunch chopped green
onions
8 ounces chopped water
chestnuts

10 ounces frozen peas (or 1
can Lesueur English peas)
1 head lettuce—shredded
2 cups mayonnaise
2 tablespoons sugar
1 jar bacon bits

Mix first five ingredients. Mix mayonnaise and sugar and pour over lettuce mixture. Cover and refrigerate. Mix well and add bacon bits.

Linda Stone
Moreland, Georgia

CORN SALAD

Yield: 4-6 servings

1 can (12 ounce size) whole
kernel corn, drained
3/4 cup diced celery
1/2 cup chopped onion
1/4 cup diced pepper (green
or red pepper)

1 teaspoon prepared mustard
3 tablespoons salad oil
1/4 cup vinegar

Mix all ingredients, chill. Serve on lettuce leaf.

Mrs. Ferrell Parrott (Emily)
Senoia, Georgia

Skill in cooking is as readily shown in a baked potato or a johnny-cake as in a canvas-back duck.

The Dixie Cook-Book (1888)

113

VIDALIA ONION-TOMATO SALAD

Yield: 5 to 6 servings

Salad:

4 ripe tomatoes, peeled and sliced

1 jumbo Vidalia onion thinly sliced and separated into rings

1/4 teaspoon fresh or dried herbs (parsley, chives, basil and dill weed)

Celery salt to taste

Salt and pepper to taste

Vinaigrette Dressing:

3/4 cup olive oil (or 1/4 cup olive oil, 1/2 cup corn, safflower, or soy oil)

1/2 teaspoon dry mustard

1 teaspoon Dijon mustard

1 cup wine vinegar

1/4 teaspoon sugar

1/2 teaspoon salt, or to taste

Pepper to taste

Salad:

On the bottom of a 13x9 pan or large bowl, spread onion rings. Cover with tomato slices in a single layer. Sprinkle tomatoes with herbs and seasonings. Cover and refrigerate. Let chill for at least 3 hours.

Vinaigrette dressing is very good with this recipe and can be added before you chill.

Dressing:

Combine oil, vinegar, mustard (both), sugar, salt and pepper in a screw top jar and shake to combine. Any unused Vinaigrette dressing can be refrigerated until ready to use. If possible, bring to room temperature before serving.

Mrs. Jewell Meltzer

CAULIFLOWER SALAD

Yield: 8 servings

1 head of lettuce
1 medium onion, chopped
1 pound of bacon, fried and broken into bite-sized pieces

1 head of cauliflower, broken into flowerettes
1 (8 ounce) package shredded cheddar cheese

DRESSING:

2 cups mayonnaise
1/4 cup sugar
1 teaspoon thyme

1 teaspoon celery seed
Trace of milk

Layer in order: 1st—head of lettuce
2nd—onion
3rd—bacon
4th—cauliflower
5th—cheese

Mix dressing ingredients together and toss with salad just before serving.

Mrs. Thomas W. Morningstar (Donna)
Sharpsburg, Georgia

We may live without poetry, music and art;
We may live without conscience, and live without heart.
We may live without friends; we may live without books;
But civilized man cannot live without cooks.

E.R. Bulwer-Lytton

115

SPINACH SALAD
Prepare early to let flavors mix

Yield: 10 servings

1 package fresh spinach
and/or watercress
1 pound of crumbled cooked
bacon
6 hard boiled eggs sliced
1 package frozen tiny peas
(slightly cooked)

1 small onion sliced
1 cup mayonnaise
1 cup yogurt plain
Salt & pepper to taste
1 cup grated swiss cheese
1 small jar pimientos

Put spinach in flat 10x13 casserole dish. Layer with 1/2 eggs and 1/2 bacon. Put 1/2 peas and 1/2 onion slices. Spread a layer of mayonnaise and yogurt (mixed)—use about one cup of mixed. Salt and pepper lightly. Repeat layers, using remainder of spinach, egg, bacon, peas, onions, and yogurt mix. Top with swiss cheese and garnish with pimientos.

Mrs. Frank Marchman (Beth Candler)

SPINACH SALAD

Yield: 5 servings

1 bag fresh spinach, washed
and drained
1 (16 ounce) can bean
sprouts, drained

1 (8 ounce) can of water
chestnuts, sliced
5 slices crisp bacon, crumbled

Dressing:

1/2 cup salad oil
1/2 cup sugar
1/2 cup vinegar
1 small onion, chopped

2 teaspoons Worcestershire
sauce
2 teaspoons Soy sauce

Toss first four ingredients. Add dressing as desired. The dressing will keep in the refrigerator.

Mrs. John Miller (Cathy)

SPINACH-ORANGE SALAD
WITH HONEY VINAIGRETTE DRESSING

Yield: 4 servings

4 cups spinach leaves
1 (11-ounce) can mandarin
orange sections, drained
1/2 cup red onions, sliced

1 (2-ounce) package slivered
almonds, toasted to light
brown

Dressing:

3 tablespoons distilled white
vinegar
3 tablespoons vegetable oil
1 tablespoon honey

1/2 teaspoon salt
Dash pepper
Dash poppy seeds
Dash celery seeds

In large salad bowl mix spinach, oranges, onions, and almonds. Pour in dressing mixture and toss. (Dressing mixture can be made ahead and kept in refrigerator for weeks. Also good on fresh fruit salad.)

Mrs. Minerva Cole Woodroof

Give no more to every guest
Than he is able to digest;
Give him always of the prime,
And but little at a time.

Swift

117

BROCCOLI SALAD

Yield: 10 to 12 servings

Salad:

2 bunches broccoli (use only flowerettes)
1 medium onion (red or sweet)

1/2 cup dark raisins
10 to 12 slices bacon, fried crisp and crumbled

Dressing:

1 cup mayonnaise
2 tablespoons vinegar

2 teaspoons sugar

Wash and dry broccoli. Toss first 4 ingredients. Combine with dressing and marinate 1 to 2 hours in refrigerator (covered). May be used immediately, but raisins become more plump when marinated first.

Mrs. Wesley Ann Simmons

RAW BROCCOLI SALAD
Delicious with ham or fried chicken

Yield: 5 servings

1 bunch fresh broccoli
4 hard boiled eggs, chopped
1 medium onion, chopped
1 small jar chopped pimiento olives

1/4 to 1 cup mayonnaise, enough to cover vegetables

Cut broccoli into small pieces (even stems that are tender). Add other ingredients and combine with mayonnaise.

Mrs. Jimmy Hutchinson (Jane)

$10,000 SALAD DRESSING

Yield: 4 to 6 servings

1/4 cup vinegar
1/2 cup sugar
1 teaspoon salt
1 teaspoon celery seed

1 teaspoon paprika
1 tablespoon grated onion
1 cup oil

Combine first six ingredients in blender. Add oil very slowly, blending constantly. Let stand 24 hours before serving.

Mrs. Carl E. Williams (Eddy)

CITY CAFÉ HOUSE DRESSING

1 clove garlic, mashed
1/2 teaspoon salt
1/2 teaspoon freshly ground
    black pepper

1 teaspoon Dijon or 1/2
    teaspoon dry mustard
Juice of one lemon

Combine ingredients above in a Dijon mustard jar. Fill the jar with your favorite oil to one inch from top (Safflower is good). Put on the top of jar and shake. Pour over salad at last minute and toss.

Jack Deyton
City Café

CELERY SEED DRESSING

2 cups Wesson Oil
1 1/4 cups sugar
2 teaspoons prepared mustard
2 teaspoons salt

2/3 cup vinegar
1 tablespoon onion juice
2 tablespoons celery seed
    (add last)

Combine sugar, salt, onion juice, mustard and 2 tablespoons vinegar. Beat well in mixer. Add oil and remaining vinegar alternately, beating well. It will thicken and become creamy. Stir in celery seed.

Mrs. Jimmy Hutchinson (Jane)

119

ROQUEFORT DRESSING

Yield: Approx. 3 Cups

1 cup mayonnaise
1 cup sour cream
6 tablespoons milk
4 tablespoons lemon juice
1 tablespoon vinegar

1 tablespoon grated onion
2 garlic cloves, minced
1 1/2 cups roquefort (or bleu cheese), crumbled

Combine all ingredients, mix well, and refrigerate 30 minutes to 1 hour before serving.

Will keep for several days refrigerated!!

BLUE CHEESE SALAD DRESSING

Yield: 4 to 6 servings

1/2 cup Hellman's Real Mayonnaise
1/2 cup of sour cream

3 tablespoons milk
2 tablespoons lemon juice
2/3 cup crumbled bleu cheese

Combine mayonnaise and sour cream. Stir in milk and lemon juice—mix well. Add bleu cheese and refrigerate overnight. This recipe can be doubled easily.

Mrs. Joe Distel (Pat)

BUTTERMILK BLUE CHEESE DRESSING

3 ounces blue cheese
7/8 cup buttermilk

1 cup mayonnaise
3/4 teaspoon garlic salt

Mix ingredients well. Store 12 hours before serving.

Mrs. Lawrence W. Keith, Jr. (Jane)

FRENCH DRESSING

3 teaspoons Lowry season salt
1 teaspoon sugar
2 tablespoons tarragon
  vinegar
2 tablespoons lemon juice
2/3 cup olive oil

Mix first four ingredients. Add oil slowly, stirring constantly.
Mrs. William M. Berry, III (Anne Jarrell)

VALLEY RANCH MIX

1 1/2 tablespoons salt
2 teaspoons parsley flakes
1 teaspoon garlic powder
1 teaspoon pepper
1/2 teaspoon onion powder

Mix these ingredients and store in refrigerator in air tight jar.

VALLEY RANCH DRESSING

Yield: 1 pint

3 1/8 teaspoons Valley Ranch
  Mix
1 cup mayonnaise
1 cup buttermilk

Combine all ingredients, mixing well. Keep refrigerated.

HERB DRESSING

1 pint Valley Ranch Dressing
1 tablespoon chopped chives
1/2 teaspoon tarragon

BLEU CHEESE DRESSING

1 pint Valley Ranch Dressing
1/4 cup Bleu cheese,
  crumbled

DILL DRESSING

1 pint Valley Ranch Dressing
Dash Worcestershire sauce
1 tablespoon dill weed

ETIQUETTE

As this is not an etiquette book, we can only give a few hints. Once seated at table, gloves are drawn off and laid in the lap under the napkin, which is spread lightly, not tucked in. Raw oysters are eaten with a fork; soup from the side of a spoon without noise, or tipping the plate. The mouth should not go to the food, but food to the mouth. Eat without noise and with the lips closed. Friends will not care to see how you masticate your food, unless they are of a very investigating turn of mind. Bread should be broken, not cut, and should be eaten by morsels, and not broken into soup or gravy. It is in bad taste to mix food on the plate. Fish must be eaten with the fork. Macaroni is cut and cheese crumbled on the plate, and eaten with a fork. Pastry should be broken and eaten with a fork, never cut with a knife. Game and chicken are cut, but never eaten with the bones held in the fingers. Oranges are peeled without breaking the inner skin, being held meantime on a fork. Pears are pared while held by the stem. Cherry-stones, or other substances which are to be removed from the mouth, are passed to the napkin held to the lips, and then returned to the plate. Salt must be left on the side of the plate, and never on the table-cloth. Cut with the knife, but never put it in the mouth; the fork must convey the food, and may be held in either hand as convenient. (Of course, when the old-fashioned two-tined fork is used, it would be absurd to practice this rule.) Food that can not be held with a fork should be eaten with a spoon. Never help yourself to butter or any other food with your own knife or fork. Never pick your teeth at table, or make any sound with the mouth in eating. Bread eaten with meat should not be buttered. Bread and butter is a dish for dessert. Eat slowly for both health and manners. Do not lean your arms on the table, or sit too far back, or lounge. Pay as little attention as possible to accidents. When asked "what do you prefer?" name some part at once. When done, lay your knife and fork side by side on the plate, with handles to the right. When you rise from your chair leave it where it stands. Of course, loud talking or boisterous conduct is entirely out of place at table, where each should appear at his best, practicing all he can of the amenities of life, and observing all he knows of the forms of good society.

The Dixie Cook-Book (1888)

E N T R E E S

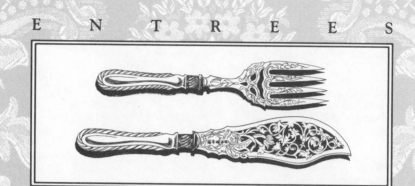

Ivory Handled Fish Serving Set

ENTREES

RARE TENDERLOIN WITH MADEIRA SAUCE

Yield: 8 servings

Oven: 450° 20 minutes

1 beef tenderloin	6 ounces soy sauce
Coarse ground black pepper	1 ounce worcestershire sauce
2 ounces Kitchen Bouquet	

Rub tenderloin with pepper and place in marinade. Let marinate several hours, turning frequently.

Place uncovered, in preheated oven. Cook 20 minutes. Turn oven off (DO NOT OPEN DOOR) and wait 15 minutes. Take meat out and let stand about 5 minutes before serving.

Madeira Sauce

1 can beef consomme	1/2 cup water
1 can beef broth	1 can (8 ounces) sliced
2 cloves garlic, pressed	mushrooms
2 stalks celery (tops only)	Lemon juice and sugar
1/2 teaspoon thyme	1/3 cup + 2 tablespoons
1 bay leaf	madeira
1 carrot	2 tablespoons corn starch
Small bunch parsley	

Process all ingredients except the last five in the food processor. Place in a sauce pan and simmer until reduced to 2/3 of original volume. Add 1/2 cup water and reduce again. Drain mushrooms, saving liquid and add mushrooms. Add lemon juice and sugar to taste. Mix 2 tablespoons cornstarch with 2 tablespoons madeira and add to sauce to thicken. Add remaining 1/3 madeira. If needed, add liquid from mushrooms.

Mrs. Frank Bassett Jarrell (Marion)
Atlanta, Georgia

BEEF TENDERLOIN WITH MUSHROOM SAUCE

Oven: 425° 45 to 60 minutes   Yield: 12 servings

1 cup bourbon
1 cup water
Juice of one lemon
2 teaspoons worcestershire
2 teaspoons Pickapepper
   sauce
1 teaspoon onion salt
1 teaspoon lemon-pepper
   seasoning
1 teaspoon paprika
1 beef tenderloin, trimmed (5
   pounds)

2 slices bacon
1/2 pound fresh mushrooms,
   sliced
1 cup water
1 1/2 teaspoons chicken-
   flavored bouillon granules
1 1/2 teaspoons beef-flavored
   bouillon granules
2 teaspoons browning and
   seasoning sauce
2 tablespoons cornstarch
1/4 cup water

Combine first 8 ingredients; stir well. Spear tenderloin in several places. Place tenderloin and marinade in a zip lock heavy duty plastic bag; seal tightly. Refrigerate 8 hours.

Drain and reserve marinade. Place tenderloin on rack of broiler pan; place bacon length wise over tenderloin. Insert meat thermometer, making sure it does not touch fat. Bake at 425° for 45 to 60 minutes or until thermometer registers 140° (rare) or 150° (medium). Baste occasionally with marinade while baking. Remove to serving platter. Reserve remaining marinade.

Pour remaining marinade in a sauce pan; cook over medium heat until reduced to 1/2 cup. Add mushrooms, 1 cup water, bouillon granules and browning and seasoning sauce; cook until mushrooms are tender. Combine cornstarch and 1/4 cup water; stir into mushroom mixture. Bring mixture to a boil; cook one minute or until thickened and bubbly, stirring constantly. Brush tenderloin with mushroom sauce. Slice tenderloin and serve with sauce.

Mrs. Walter M. Lonergan, II (Ginny)

BARBECUE BRISKET

Oven: 300° 5 hours   Yield: 6 to 10 servings

One 2 to 3 lb. beef brisket   Few drops Liquid Smoke
  (fresh)   2 tablespoons vinegar
3/4 cup catsup   1 teaspoon paprika
1 tablespoon worcestershire   3/4 cup water
  sauce   1/4 to 1/2 cup sugar
1 tablespoon salt   2 to 3 onions, sliced

    Place meat in foil. Slice onions and place over meat. Combine remaining ingredients and pour over meat. Wrap tightly in foil and bake 5 hours at 300°. Cool and slice. Then reheat with more sauce or serve warm from oven with sauce.

Mrs. Robert Teller (Nancy)

BRAISED BEEF TIPS

Yield: 4 to 6 servings

1 pound well trimmed sirloin   1 tablespoon teriyaki sauce
1 tablespoon seasoned   1 teaspoon soy sauce
  tenderizer   1 medium onion, chopped
1 teaspoon garlic powder   1/4 teaspoon sugar
2 tablespoons cooking oil   1/4 cup cooking sherry
1/2 cup water

    Cut sirloin in strips 1/4 inch thick and 2 inches long. Sprinkle with tenderizer and garlic powder. Pierce meat with fork. Let stand 30 minutes.

    Brown meat in skillet with cooking oil. Add all of the other ingredients. Simmer 20 minutes.

    Serve over rice or noodles. Enjoy!

Mr. Carlton Ingram

STANLEY'S BEEF TIPS

Oven: 300° 1 to 1 1/2 hours | Yield: 4 to 6 servings

2 lb. beef tips (can use stew
  beef chunks)
1 can French onion soup
1/2 can water

1 tablespoon soy sauce
1 tablespoon worcestershire
  sauce

Sprinkle tips with tenderizer. Place in an oven baking bag. Mix soup, water and seasonings and pour over meat in bag. Fasten bag, puncture top of bag with a fork. Bake at 300° for 1 hour to 1 1/2 hours. Serve over rice.

Mrs. Stanley Cauthen (Mary Ann)

STEAK ROLL-UPS

Yield: 4 servings

1 package Lipton's dry onion
  soup mix
2 tablespoons water
3 tablespoons spicy brown
  mustard

1 small can B&B garlic
  mushrooms
4 tablespoons melted butter
4 large cubed steaks
pepper

Mix soup mix and water. Let stand a few minutes then mix with mustard.

Spread mixture on cubed steak sprinkled with pepper. Add mushrooms then roll up and hold in place with toothpicks. Brush with melted butter. Broil 6 minutes. Turn over, brush with butter and broil 6 more minutes.

Anita Royal

"Unquiet meals make ill digestions."

Shakespeare

BEEF ROUND ROAST

Oven: 350° 1 to 1 1/2 hours   Yield: 6 to 8 servings

2 sticks butter or margarine
1 medium onion, chopped
6 green onions, chopped
2 teaspoons garlic, chopped
1 tablespoon parsley
1 can cream of mushroom
  soup

1 1/2 cups Italian bread
  crumbs
Salt to taste
Pepper to taste
2 beef rounds
1 cup water

Sauté onion, green onion, garlic and parsley in one stick of butter. Add cream of mushroom soup and 1/2 can of water to seasonings. Add bread crumbs and mix well. Melt one stick of butter, adding salt and pepper. Spread this butter mixture on beef rounds. Place one beef round in baking dish. Spread dressing mixture on top of round. Place second round on top of dressing. Fasten together with toothpicks. Pour one cup water in baking dish. Cover with foil and bake at 350° for 1 to 1 1/2 hours. Raw new potatoes and raw carrot slices may be placed around beef before baking, if desired.

Gayle Ordoyne
Senoia, Georgia

He may live without books—what is knowledge but
   grieving?
He may live without hope—what is hope but deceiving?
He may live without love—what is passion but pining?
But where is the man that can live without dining?

Owen Meredith

BEEF AND NOODLE CASSEROLE
Quick and easy

Oven: 350° 40 minutes   Yield: 6 to 8 servings

1 pound ground beef
1 large onion, chopped
2 cloves garlic, minced
1/2 cup bell pepper, chopped
1 (4 ounce) can green peas,
   drained
1 (16 ounce) can tomatoes,
   drained and chopped
1 (6 ounce) can sliced
   mushrooms, drained

1 can cheddar cheese soup
1 (8 ounce) package noodles,
   cooked and drained
1 tablespoon worcestershire
   sauce
Dash of hot sauce
Salt and pepper to taste
1/2 to 1 cup grated cheese

In a large skillet, brown ground beef, onion, garlic and pepper. Drain. Combine with remaining ingredients (except cheese). Place in 9x13" pan and bake at 350° for 40 minutes. Top with cheese after removing from oven.

Mrs. Henry Sewell (Lucy)

CHURRASCO DE NICARAGUA
From the Las Mercedes Hotel, Nicaragua

Yield: 4 servings

4 filet mignon - 3" thick
4 fresh garlic cloves, peeled
   and finely minced

Olive oil
One bunch fresh (not dried)
   chives, finely chopped

Place filet on cutting board and cut *with the grain* approximately 3/4 inches thick, rolling and cutting until the steak is roughly 3/4" thick by 8" long. Score 1/8" deep on both sides, but on one side with the grain and the other side against the grain. Apply olive oil generously on both sides. Rub minced garlic and chives with fingers against the scoring allowing both to enter the cut areas.

Place in glass baking dish, cover with Saran, and store in refrigerator to marinate for 4 to 10 hours. Allow to come to room temperature, then cook to medium rare or to taste on a very hot grill.

John C. Dunn

MEAT WHIRL

Oven: 350° 1 hour   Yield: 6 to 8 servings

1 1/2 pounds ground chuck
1 cup soft breadcrumbs
1 egg
2 teaspoons mustard
1 1/2 teaspoons salt
1 heaping teaspoon
  horseradish

1/8 teaspoon pepper
1 can (8 ounces) tomato
  sauce
1 1/2 cups shredded cheddar
  cheese (sharp)
1 teaspoon dill seed

In a bowl lightly mix meat, crumbs, egg, mustard, salt, horseradish, pepper and 1/4 cup tomato sauce, reserving remaining tomato sauce. On wax paper pat meat into a 10x4" rectangular form and sprinkle with cheese. Roll from shorter end as for jelly roll. Press ends to seal. Carefully transfer to baking dish, seam side down. Bake at 350° for 45 minutes. Pour remaining tomato sauce over the meat. Sprinkle with dill seed. Bake additional 15 minutes. Let stand for 10 minutes and remove to a warm platter.

Mrs. Charlie Adams (Jeanene)

If girls were taught to take as much genuine pride in dusting a room well, hanging a curtain gracefully, or broiling a steak to a nicety, as they feel when they have mastered one of Mozart's or Beethoven's grand symphonies, there would be fewer complaining husbands and unhappy wives.

The Dixie Cook-Book (1888)

DR. MATHEWS' SAN FRANCISCO SPECIAL

Yield: 4 to 5 servings

1 pound ground beef
Salt, pepper, and garlic salt
  (to taste)
1 (10 ounce) package frozen
  spinach
2 medium onions, chopped

2 or 3 medium eggs
1 small can (2 ounce)
  mushrooms (diced or
  sliced)
1/2 cup grated Monterey Jack
  cheese

Brown and drain meat. Season to taste with salt, pepper, and garlic salt. Cook spinach according to package directions. Add to meat mixture along with the chopped onions. Cook over medium heat until onions become translucent. Stir in eggs, one at a time. Add drained mushrooms and mix well. Top with grated cheese.

Serve with hot garlic bread and green salad.

Rosemary B. Mathews
Monroe, Georgia

✓BEANS & RICE WITH BEEF

Yield: ~~4 to 5~~ 3-4 servings

3/4 ~~1 1/2~~ cups pinto beans
  (soaked a few hours)
3 ~~6~~ cups water
1 onion, chopped
1 teaspoon salt
1/2 teaspoon black pepper

1 can tomato sauce
1/2 ~~1~~ tablespoon shortening
1 ~~1 1/2~~ pounds ground beef
1 ~~2~~ cups rice (cooked in salted
  water)

Let beans, onion, shortening with seasonings boil until beans are tender. Add tomato sauce and cook until well mixed. Add ground beef slightly browned in oil to the beans. Add cooked rice, which has been allowed to dry, to the mixture. (For a quickie—use 2 cans pinto beans instead of dry beans.)

Mrs. Thomas Fox (Emily)
Senoia, Georgia

132

MEAT BALLS STROGANOFF

Yield: 6 to 8 servings

1 1/2 pounds ground chuck
3/4 cup milk
3/4 cup dried bread crumbs
1 teaspoon salt
1 teaspoon pepper
3 tablespoons snipped parsley
1/4 cup margarine
3/4 cup minced onion
1/2 pound mushrooms (sliced)

3/4 teaspoons paprika
2 tablespoons flour
1 can condensed beef
   bouillon, undiluted
1/2 teaspoon worcestershire
1/2 cup sour cream
hot fluffy rice
snipped fresh dill

With fork combine ground chuck, milk, bread crumbs, salt, pepper and parsley. Shape into 1 1/4 inch balls. Sauté balls in 2 tablespoons butter in skillet until brown. Remove and reserve. Add 2 tablespoons more of butter to skillet and sauté onions and mushrooms with paprika until tender (about 5 minutes). Sprinkle flour over mushroom mixture and stir. Continue stirring and slowly add bouillon. Return meat balls to sauce, cover and simmer for 10 minutes. Just before serving stir in worcestershire sauce and sour cream. Serve with hot rice sprinkled with dill.

Mrs. R.O. Jones II (Evelyn)

✓ HAMBURGER STROGANOFF

3-4
Yield: 8 servings

4 strips bacon
1 ~~1 1/2 to 2~~ pounds ground
   beef, lean
1 small onion
1 ~~two~~ cans cream of
   mushroom soup

1/4 ~~1/2~~ teaspoon paprika
1/4 ~~1/3 to 1/2~~ cup sour cream
Noodles - 1 cup

Fry bacon and crumble. Brown ground beef with onion. Mix in bacon, soup and paprika and simmer, uncovered, for 20 minutes. Add sour cream and heat thoroughly. Serve over hot buttered noodles with French bread and a tossed salad.

Mrs. John Andrews (Pat)

133

FAVORITE MEATLOAF

Yield: 6 servings

1 (8 ounce) can tomato sauce
1/4 cup brown sugar
1 teaspoon prepared mustard
2 eggs, lightly beaten
1 medium onion, minced

1/4 cup cracker crumbs
2 pounds lean ground beef
1 1/2 teaspoons salt
1/4 teaspoon pepper

In small bowl, combine tomato sauce, brown sugar and mustard and set aside. In large mixing bowl, combine eggs, onion, cracker crumbs, ground beef, salt and pepper. Add 1/2 cup tomato sauce mixture and stir thoroughly. Place meat mixture in glass ring mold or 2-quart microproof round casserole. Pour remaining tomato sauce over top of meat. Cook uncovered on HIGH 12 to 14 minutes. Let stand covered 5 to 10 minutes before serving.

Mrs. Gene A. Terrell (Joyce)

MEAT LOAF

Oven: 350° 1 hour

Yield: 6 servings

2 lbs. ground beef
1/2 cup chopped onion
1/4 cup chopped bell pepper
1 teaspoon salt
1/4 teaspoon pepper
2 eggs

1 can condensed tomato soup
1/4 cup milk
1 tablespoon worcestershire
sauce
1 1/2 cups cornflake crumbs
1 cup grated cheese

Combine all ingredients and mix well. Pour mixture into flat oven dish and shape into loaf, packing lightly together. Do not let meat touch sides of pan. Bake at 350° for an hour. Cover loosely with foil while baking.

Mrs. Thomas Fox (Emily)

MUSHROOM-FILLED MEATLOAF

Oven: 350° 1 hour   Yield: 6 servings

2 cups fresh mushrooms,
  sliced
1 cup chopped onion
2 tablespoons margarine
1/2 cup sour cream
2 eggs
1/2 cup milk

1 1/2 pounds ground beef
3/4 cup fresh soft bread
  crumbs
2 teaspoons salt
1 tablespoon worcestershire
  sauce

Sour Cream Sauce:

1 cup sour cream
1 teaspoon mustard
1 teaspoon prepared
  horseradish

1/2 teaspoon salt
Dash of nutmeg
Dash of white pepper

In a saucepan, sauté 1 cup mushrooms and onions in margarine. Remove from heat and stir in sour cream. Set aside. In separate bowl, combine eggs, milk, ground beef, bread crumbs, salt and worcestershire sauce. Place half of mixture in a 9x5x3" loaf pan. Make trough in center of meat and fill with mushroom mixture. Shape rest of meat over filling, making sure all filling is covered. Seal well around edges. Bake at 350° for 1 hour. Let stand 15 minutes before slicing. Garnish with remaining mushrooms. Combine sauce ingredients in saucepan and heat over low heat. Serve with meatloaf.

Mrs. Kenny Coggin (Susan)

"Sit down and feed, and welcome to our table."

Shakespeare

135

CORNED BEEF CASSEROLE
Freezes well

Oven: 350° 15 to 20 minutes   Yield: 6 to 8 servings

1 (8 ounce) package spaghetti
(cooked and drained)
1 (12 ounce) can corned beef
(chopped)
1 can cream of chicken soup
2 cups evaporated milk

1 cup grated sharp cheddar
cheese
1/2 cup chopped onion
1 stick margarine (melted)
Salt and pepper to taste
1 cup bread crumbs

Spray 13"x9" oven proof dish with Pam. Mix all ingredients together reserving 1/4 cup cheddar cheese and bread crumbs. Pour into pan and sprinkle with remaining cheese and bread crumbs. Bake at 350° for 15 to 20 minutes.

Mrs. Stanley Cauthen (Mary Ann)

CORNED BEEF WITH ORANGE-MUSTARD GLAZE

Oven: 350° 30 minutes   Yield: 6 to 8 servings

3/4 pound corned beef
3/4 cup orange marmalade

3 tablespoons Dijon mustard
3 tablespoons brown sugar

Put corned beef in a large pot of water. Bring to a boil, then simmer very slowly at least 3 hours, until tender. Remove from pot, drain, and place in a 2 quart casserole dish.

Mix together marmalade, mustard and brown sugar and pour over meat. Bake uncovered for 30 minutes at 350°.

Mrs. William M. Berry, III (Anne)

CHASTAIN TOMATOES
Great at an outdoor picnic!

Yield: 6 servings

6 sliced tomatoes
Sliced mozzarella cheese (6 oz. package)

Good Seasons Italian Dressing (package made up)
Basil leaves, chopped

In the serving dish alternate slices of cheese and tomatoes overlapping slightly spiraling to the center. Pour prepared dressing over tomatoes and cheese and sprinkle chopped basil on top. Marinate 6 hours to overnight.

Anne Watkins
Atlanta, Ga.

TOMATOES PROVENCAL
This is a good way to spice up bland winter tomatoes.

Yield: 4 servings

1 tablespoon Dijon mustard
1/2 teaspoon sugar
1/2 teaspoon pepper
Juice of 1 lemon
1/2 cup vinegar

4 tablespoons butter
1 bunch spring onions (tops only)
2 firm large sliced tomatoes

Melt butter. Mix in mustard, sugar, lemon, pepper, and vinegar. Heat to boiling. Can hold at this point and reheat when ready to pour over sliced tomatoes, and top with sliced green onions. If tomatoes are mealy, can heat for a few minutes in oven or microwave. Be careful not to overcook or tomatoes will disintegrate. Do not add salt until served, makes tomatoes watery.

This dish is good with rare roast beef or chicken casserole.

Mrs. Delia T. Crouch

CAULIFLOWER AU GRATIN

Oven: 375° 20 to 30 minutes　　　　　　Yield: 8 to 10 servings

1 large head cauliflower
6 tablespoons butter
3 tablespoons flour
Salt and pepper
2 cups milk
1 cup sharp cheddar cheese

4 tablespoons parsley
1 tablespoon chopped sweet
　onion
1/8 teaspoon dry mustard
Corn flakes or cheese crackers
Paprika

Break cauliflower into flowerettes, soak in cold water 30 minutes. Cook in salted boiling water 10 minutes. Drain. Blend butter and flour over low heat. Salt and pepper to taste. Add cold milk, cook and stir to a smooth sauce over medium heat. Add 1 cup sharp cheddar cheese, parsley, onion and dry mustard. Pour a small amount of sauce in bottom of casserole then a layer of cauliflower. Continue to layer. Crumble small amount of corn flakes or cheese crackers and sprinkle on top. Shake paprika all over. Bake 375° for 20 to 30 minutes until hot and bubbly.

Mrs. Eugene Craven (Pat)

CELERY CASSEROLE

Oven: 350° 45 minutes　　　　　　　　　　Yield: 6 servings

4 cups diced celery
1 can cream of celery soup,
　undiluted
1 6 ounce can water
　chestnuts, sliced
1/4 cup sliced almonds

Small can of pimientos
Buttered breadcrumbs
Dash or two Worcestershire
　sauce—for fish and light
　foods

Cook celery slightly until fairly soft. Drain, add soup, water chestnuts, pimientos and almonds. Dust with bread crumbs.

Mrs. Jett Fisher (Carol)

JOHN'S RED CABBAGE
Goes well with pork and turkey dishes.

Yield: 6 to 8 servings

1/2 stick margarine
1 average size head red
cabbage
1/8 cup dehydrated chopped
onion
1 teaspoon black pepper or to
taste

Dash salt
1/8 cup bacon bits
1/4 cup Worcestershire sauce
1/4 cup A-1 sauce
1/8 cup vinegar

Melt margarine in sauce pan or skillet, add cabbage, onion, black pepper and bacon bits. Sauté 6 to 7 minutes, then add remaining ingredients and cover and simmer until tender, stirring occasionally.

Mrs. John J. Cenkner (Sandra)

ORIENTAL VEGETABLE DISH

Oven: 350° for 10 to 15 minutes   Yield: 8 to 10 servings

2 packages frozen peas
1/2 cup celery, chopped fine
1/2 cup onion, chopped fine
18 ounce box fresh
mushrooms
1 stick butter
1 can bean sprouts

1 can water chestnuts
4 teaspoons soy sauce
1 can cream of mushroom
soup
Topping—1/4 pound grated
cheddar cheese, 1 can
French fried onions

Cook peas according to package directions. Sauté onion, celery and mushrooms in stick of butter and mix with peas. Add bean sprouts with water chestnuts and soy sauce. Pour soup over all and mix well. Put into buttered casserole dish. Put topping on, bake 350° for 10 to 15 minutes.

Mrs. Frank Parham (Jackie Cordle)
Ringgold, GA

189

GRILLED SUMMER VEGETABLES

A delightful and easy way to prepare vegetables for your summer dining pleasure. Serve chilled with a marinade or hot with a shallot herb butter.

Yield: serves 6

1/4 cup olive oil
2 onions (Georgia vidalias of course!)
1 medium zucchini, cut lengthwise
1 red or orange pepper, cut in 1" lengths

1 yellow squash, cut lengthwise
1 sweet potato or yam prebaked, sliced 1/2" thick
1 small eggplant, sliced 1/2" thick

Clean and prepare vegetables individually. Set vegetables on grill and watch closely remembering that the denser vegetables will take longer to cook so put them on first. The precooked potato or yam will only take about 5 minutes. When vegetables have reached desired doneness, remove from grill directly into marinade or serve hot with shallot butter.

MARINADE FOR CHILLED GRILLED VEGETABLES

5 fresh garlic cloves
2 sprigs fresh rosemary
2 sprigs fresh lemon thyme

1 tablespoon extra virgin olive oil
2 tablespoons taragon vinegar
Cracked black pepper and salt

Peel garlic and chop coarsely. Whip into remaining ingredients with food processor. Let mixture sit at room temperature for at least an hour for flavors to develop.

SHALLOT-HERB BUTTER

1 small shallot, minced
1 sprig fresh oregano, chopped

1 sprig fresh thyme, chopped
4 oz. butter (1 stick)
Salt and pepper to taste

Sauté shallots and herbs in a small amount of butter. Remove from heat and add remaining butter and stir until it has all blended with the herbs and shallots. Replace on heat and wait until butter is frothing. Remove from heat before the butter browns. Spoon off froth until butter is clear. Serve over grilled vegetables.

John Ehrenhard

HOT GERMAN POTATO SALAD

Oven: 350° for 30 minutes   Yield: 10 to 12 servings

8 medium sized red potatoes   2/3 cup water
6 slices bacon   2/3 cup vinegar
1 cup chopped onion   1 tablespoon salt
1 cup chopped celery   2/3 cup sugar
3 tablespoons flour

Boil potatoes until tender. Drain off water and set aside to cool. Fry bacon until crisp, reserving 1/4 cup grease. In large skillet sauté onion and celery in bacon grease until opaque, about 2 minutes. Sprinkle with flour and stir. Add water and vinegar, stirring until mixture boils. Stir in salt and sugar and remove from heat. Peel potatoes and slice into 2 quart baking dish. Pour on dressing, add crumbled bacon and mix lightly. Bake uncovered at 350° for 30 minutes.

Mrs. Mike Spitler (Rita)

OVEN-FRIED POTATOES

Oven: 375° 45 minutes   Yield: 6 to 8 servings

3 medium potatoes (scrubbed   1/2 teaspoon salt
  and cut into 1/8" slices)   1/4 teaspoon garlic powder
1/4 cup vegetable oil   1/4 teaspoon paprika
1 tablespoon parmesan cheese   1/4 teaspoon pepper

Place potatoes in 13x9x2" pan in a single layer, slightly overlapping. Combine remaining ingredients. Brush potatoes with 1/2 oil mixture. Bake, uncovered, at 375° for 45 minutes, basting occasionally with the rest of the oil mixture.

Mrs. Stanley Lanier (Debbie)

191

CURRIED POTATOES
An Indian recipe

Yield: 8 servings

4 to 5 pounds new potatoes
(do not peel)
1 tablespoon poppy seeds
6 tablespoons olive oil
2 teaspoons cumin seeds
1 or 2 teaspoons minced
garlic (prepared)

1 tablespoon (or 2 if you
really like curry powder)
1 teaspoon salt
1 teaspoon pepper
2 cups diced onions
1 teaspoon lemon juice

Cook and drain new potatoes. Heat poppy seeds in olive oil until they start to pop. Combine the rest of the seasonings in olive oil and sauté onions in this mixture. Pour this in with the potatoes and mash together. Mix in lemon juice with this. If potatoes are not still warm, heat in casserole dish at 350° for about 15 to 20 minutes until hot.

Dr. Cliff A. Cranford, Jr.

LOUISE'S TWICE-BAKED POTATOES

One potato per serving
Butter
Milk

Cheddar cheese
Salt & pepper
Paprika

Bake potatoes until well done. Cut small opening in top of potato, scoop out inside of potato into a bowl. Mash and add butter and milk, salt and pepper to taste. Add a little cheddar cheese. Replace mixture into potato shell and sprinkle with paprika.

Return to oven (temp 350°) for 15 to 20 minutes before serving.

Lewis Grizzard
Atlanta, GA

SWEET POTATO CUSTARD PIE OR SOUFFLÉ

Oven: 375° 30 to 45 minutes   Yield: 1 pie

3 medium sweet potatoes
   (about 2 1/2 cups mashed)
1 cup sugar
1/2 pint sour cream
1 teaspoon vanilla
1 1/2 sticks butter or
   margarine

1 can Angel Flake coconut
Nutmeg (optional)
Cinnamon (optional)
Raisins (souffle)
Miniature marshmallows
   (soufflé)

Pie: Boil sweet potatoes with skin until tender. Drain and peel potatoes. Mash potatoes and add remaining ingredients. Put in unbaked pie shell and bake at 375° for 30 to 45 minutes.

Soufflé: Prepare as above, except add raisins and marshmallows and bake in casserole. Cook until almost done and put more marshmallows on top and brown.

Bobbie Hammock

BULGAR WHEAT CASSEROLE

Oven: 350° 40 minutes   Yield: 6 servings

2 tablespoons margarine or
   oil
1 small onion, chopped fine
1/2 green pepper, chopped
   fine
1 cup sliced mushrooms
1 cup bulgar wheat

1 cube beef bouillon
2 1/2 cups water
1 tablespoon chopped parsley
1 1/2 teaspoons rosemary
1/2 teaspoon thyme
1/2 teaspoon sage
1/2 teaspoon salt

Sauté onion, mushrooms and pepper in margarine. When done, stir in one cup bulgar wheat. Mix bouillon and water. Slowly add the broth to wheat mixture. Bring all to a boil. Remove from heat. Add spices. Put in covered one quart casserole. Bake 350° for 40 minutes.

Mrs. Frank Marchman (Beth Candler)
Sharpsburg, Georgia

TAN RICE

Oven: 350° 1 hour   Yield: 6 servings

1 cup Uncle Ben's rice   1/2 cup sherry
1 tablespoon olive oil
1 (10 1/2 ounce) can
   consomme

   Pour rice into a one quart casserole dish and coat rice with olive oil. Pour in consomme and sherry. Cover and cook 350° for one hour.

Mrs. Frank Marchman (Beth Candler)
Sharpsburg, Georgia

GREEN RICE CASSEROLE

Oven: 350° 30 minutes   Yield: 10 servings

2 cups milk   2 cups grated parmesan
4 tablespoons butter or   cheese or any white cheese
   margarine   1 cup chopped parsley
4 tablespoons flour   1 cup green pepper, chopped
1 1/2 teaspoons salt   1 1/2 cups chopped green
1/2 teaspoon worcestershire   onions (tops too)
1/8 teaspoon pepper   3 cups cooked rice
Dash red pepper   1 small jar stuffed olives,
1 garlic clove, minced   sliced and drained

   Make white sauce of first 3 ingredients. Add all seasonings and cheese, blend well. Add rice and chopped vegetables. Pour in greased 2 quart casserole. Can be mixed and placed in refrigerator over night. Bake at 350° for 30 minutes. Top with buttered bread crumbs (optional).

Margaret Askew

MUSHROOM-RICE CASSEROLE

Oven: 350° 1 hour   Yield: 6 servings

1 stick butter, melted　　　　　**1 can sliced mushrooms**
1 can onion soup　　　　　　　　　**(drained)**
1 can beef consommé　　　　　　**1 cup uncooked rice**

    Mix all ingredients in 8 or 9 inch round casserole dish. Bake 1 hour uncovered at 350°.

Laura E. Brooks

ARTICHOKE AND MUSHROOM CASSEROLE

Oven: 350° 20 minutes   Yield: 8 servings

2 boxes (9 ounces) frozen　　　**1 can mushroom soup**
**　artichoke hearts (Birdseye)**　**3 tablespoons dry sherry or**
1 pound fresh mushrooms,　　　　**　wine**
**　sliced**　　　　　　　　　　　　　　　**1/2 teaspoon pepper**
1/4 cup margarine　　　　　　　　　**Parmesan cheese**

    Cook artichoke hearts by directions on box. Sauté mushrooms in butter and drain. Combine and add soup, sherry and pepper. Sprinkle top with parmesan cheese and cook.

Mrs. Billy Murphy (Francis)

If you don't have a steamer, you can substitute with a colander or strainer over a pot of boiling water.

HOT FRUIT

Oven: 350°   Yield: 10 to 12 servings

1 stick butter
1/2 cup brown sugar
2 tablespoons flour
1 cup sherry or orange juice

8 cups assorted canned fruits,
    drained (apricots, pears,
    peaches, spiced apple rings,
    chunk pineapple, cherries)

Cook first four ingredients to a sauce. Pour over mixed fruit and refrigerate overnight. Bake in 350° oven until fruit is hot and bubbly.

Mrs. Robert Chiostergi (Ginny)
Cynthia Robertson

HOT PINEAPPLE CASSEROLE

Oven: 350° for 30 minutes   Yield: 8 servings

2 cans chunk pineapple
    (15 1/2 ounce)
3/4 cup sugar

3 tablespoons flour
3 tablespoons pineapple juice

Mix the 3 ingredients above and add to pineapple.

2 cups grated cheese
1 roll Ritz crackers, crushed

1 stick butter—melted

Put pineapple mixture in 2 quart casserole, rectangular shape. Put cheese on top, next crushed crackers. Pour melted butter over all. Cook approximately 30 minutes at 350° until mixture bubbles.

Emily T. Sealy

CRANBERRY—APPLE CASSEROLE
May be used as dessert served with whipped cream.
Delicious with turkey or ham

Oven: 300° for 1 hour   Yield: 8 servings

3 cups chopped apples
1 cup white sugar
2 cups raw cranberries
   (chopped in food processor)
1/2 cup brown sugar

1 stick margarine
1/2 cup flour
1 cup regular oatmeal
1/2 cup chopped nuts

Preheat oven to 300°. Combine first three ingredients and pour into 9x13" pan. Mix together the remaining five ingredients and spread over fruit mixture and bake in 300° oven for one hour.

Mrs. Wright Lipford (Faye)

When cooking, increase protein value of foods by using:

2 tablespoons wheat germ per 1 cup flour
add dry milk powder to flour
add cheese, hard-boiled eggs, or nuts to casseroles
use a sauce made with milk

GENERAL SUGGESTIONS

On Monday, wash: Tuesday, iron: Wednesday, bake and scrub kitchen and pantry: Thursday, clean the silver-ware, examine the pots and kettles, and look after store-room and cellar: Friday, devote to general sweeping and dusting: Saturday, bake and scrub kitchen and pantry floors, and prepare for Sunday. When the clothes are folded off the frame after ironing, examine each piece to see that none are laid away that need a button or a stitch. Clean all the silver on the last Friday of each month, and go through each room and closet to see if things are kept in order and nothing going to waste. Have the sitting-room tidied up every night before retiring. Make the most of your brain and your eyes, and let no one dare tell you that you are devoting yourself to a low sphere of action. Keep cool and self-possessed. Work done *quietly* about the house seems easier. A slamming of oven doors, and the rattle and clatter of dishes, tire and bewilder every body about the house. Those who accomplish much in housekeeping—and the same is true of every other walk in life—are the quiet workers.

The Dixie Cook-Book (1888)

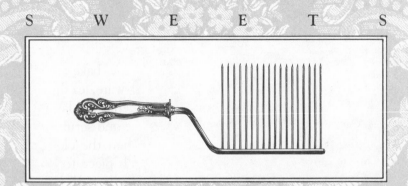

Angel Food Cake Server

Pierces and breaks the cake, preventing
mashing by pressure from a knife.

SWEETS

PINA COLADA CAKE
Delicious served warm with coffee!

Oven: 350° 35 to 40 minutes   Yield: 12 servings

2 eggs
2 cups sugar
2 cups all-purpose flour
1 can (13 1/2 ounce) drained, crushed pineapple
1 1/2 teaspoons baking soda
1 cup chopped pecans, divided into 1/2 cup portions
3/4 cup coconut, flaked

Icing:

1 (8 ounce) package cream cheese, softened
1 stick butter, softened
1 1/2 cups powdered sugar

Pre-heat oven to 350°. Mix all cake ingredients together. Bake in 9x13 greased Pyrex dish for 35 to 40 minutes.

Mix icing ingredients and ice cake while hot. Sprinkle 1/2 cup of pecans and coconut on top.

Mrs. Anne Arnold

APRICOT NECTAR POUND CAKE

Oven: 300° 50 minutes   Yield: 9-10 servings

4 eggs
3/4 cup oil
3/4 cup apricot nectar
1 tablespoon lemon flavoring
1 box white cake mix
1 box lemon gelatin

Beat eggs well. Beat in oil slowly, then apricot nectar and lemon flavoring. Next beat in cake mix and lemon gelatin. Pour in a greased bundt pan. Bake at 300° about 50 minutes. Cool cake on a rack about 15 or 20 minutes.

ICING:
1 cup powdered sugar
1 teaspoon apricot nectar
Juice of one lemon

Mix and spoon over cake.

Mrs. Jimmy Hutchinson (Jane)

201

APPLE PECAN CAKE
Can be made 2 to 3 days ahead of time

Oven: 350° 1 hour 20 minutes

3 cups all-purpose flour
1 teaspoon soda
1 teaspoon salt
1 cup vegetable oil
3 eggs
2 1/4 cups sugar

2 teaspoons vanilla
2 cups chopped pecans
3 cups peeled, chopped
   cooking apples
1/2 cup flaked coconut

Glaze:

2/3 cup firmly packed light
   brown sugar

1/4 cup milk
1/2 cup butter

Preheat oven to 350°. Combine flour, soda, and salt: mix well and set aside. Combine oil, eggs, sugar, and vanilla; beat at medium speed of electric mixer for 2 minutes. Add flour mixture; mix at lower speed just until blended. Fold in pecans, apples, and coconut. (Batter will be stiff).

Spoon into a greased and floured 10-inch tube pan. Bake at 350° for 1 hour and 20 minutes or until cake tests done. Cool in pan 10 minutes. Remove from pan; immediately drizzle glaze over cake.

GLAZE: Combine all ingredients in a heavy saucepan; bring to a full boil and cook, stirring constantly, for 2 minutes. Let cool to lukewarm.

Mrs. Joe Distel (Pat)

"'How long does getting thin take?'
Pooh asked anxiously."

A.A. Milne

BUTTERSCOTCH APPLE CAKE

Oven: 325° 1 hour   Yield: 1 cake

1 cup oil
2 cups sugar
2 eggs
2 1/3 cups plain flour
1 teaspoon cinnamon
1 teaspoon soda

1 teaspoon baking powder
3 cups apples, peeled and
  chopped
1 cup chopped nuts
1 package butterscotch
  morsels

Mix together oil, sugar and eggs. Sift together flour, cinnamon, soda and baking powder. Add chopped apples and nuts. Pour into greased 9x13 pan and sprinkle with butterscotch morsels. Bake at 325° for 1 hour.

Mrs. Larry Taylor (Barbara)

BLACKBERRY CAKE

Oven: 375° 35 to 45 minutes   Yield: 15 servings

2 1/4 cups sugar
2 teaspoons allspice
2 teaspoons nutmeg
2 teaspoons cinnamon
1 cup butter, melted
2 eggs

1/2 cup buttermilk
3 cups flour
2 teaspoons soda
1/4 teaspoon salt
2 cups blackberries

Preheat oven to 375°. Combine sugar and spices. Add melted butter and mix well. Beat in whole eggs and buttermilk. Sift flour, soda and salt and add about 1/3 to above mixture. Fold in blackberries and then fold in remaining flour mixture. Pour into well-greased pan and bake for 35 to 45 minutes. DO NOT OVER-BAKE.

When cool, frost with caramel icing. (You may also use a cream cheese frosting.)

Mrs. Goldie Fannin
Colcord, West Virginia

BANANA SPLIT CAKE

Yield: 16 servings

1 pint vanilla ice cream
3/4 cup California walnuts,
  finely chopped
1/2 cup graham cracker
  crumbs
1 stick butter or margarine,
  softened
1 cup sugar
1/2 cup cocoa

1 cup heavy or whipping
  cream
1 teaspoon vanilla extract
4 ripe medium bananas
Lemon juice
1 pint chocolate ice cream
1 pint strawberry ice cream
6 maraschino cherries

Place vanilla ice cream in refrigerator to soften slightly, about 40 minutes. (IMPORTANT: DO NOT let ice cream melt when preparing layers, only SOFTEN, or ice cream will not harden properly and you will have a real mess.) Meanwhile, finely chop 1/2 cup walnuts (reserving remaining 1/4 cup for garnish). In 9x3 inch springform pan, combine chopped walnuts, graham cracker crumbs, 3 tablespoons butter or margarine and 2 tablespoons sugar. With fingers, press mixture to bottom of pan. Evenly spread vanilla ice cream on top of crust; freeze until firm (about 45 minutes).

While waiting for vanilla ice cream to harden, in 2-quart saucepan over medium heat, cook cocoa, 1/2 cup heavy or whipping cream, 3/4 cup sugar and 4 tablespoons butter or margarine until mixture is smooth and boils, stirring constantly. Remove saucepan from heat; stir in vanilla extract. Cool fudge sauce to room temperature.

Split 3 bananas lengthwise and dip in lemon juice. Remove pan from freezer. Pour fudge sauce over vanilla ice cream; top with split bananas. Return cake to freezer; freeze 1 hour or until fudge sauce is firm. Place chocolate ice cream in refrigerator to soften slightly (about 40 minutes).

Spread chocolate ice cream over fudge and bananas. Return cake to freezer; freeze about 20 minutes to harden slightly. Remove strawberry ice cream from container to medium bowl; let stand at room temperature, stirring occasionally until it reaches a smooth spreading consistency, but not melted. Spread strawberry ice cream over chocolate ice cream. Cover and freeze until firm (about 3 hours).

TO SERVE: With fingers, break reserved 1/4 cup walnuts into small pieces. In small bowl with mixer at medium speed, beat remaining 1/2 cup heavy or whipping cream until soft peaks form. Cut remaining banana diagonally into slices and dip in lemon juice. Dip knife or metal spatula in hot water and run around edge of springform pan to loosen ice cream. Remove side of pan. Spread top of cake with whipped cream. Arrange banana slices, cherries, and broken walnuts on whipped cream.

Mrs. Kurt Witter (Lane)

FRENCH CHOCOLATE CAKE

Oven: 350° 20 to 30 minutes

1/2 cup cocoa	1/2 teaspoon baking soda
3/4 cup boiling water	1/2 cup sour cream
1/2 cup butter	2 cups flour
2 cups sugar	1/3 teaspoon salt
1 teaspoon vanilla	3 egg whites, beaten

Quick Chocolate Icing:

7 tablespoons milk	1 tablespoon Karo syrup
2 squares chocolate, unsweetened	1 stick butter
1 1/2 cups sugar	1 teaspoon vanilla

Dissolve cocoa in hot water and cool. Cream butter and sugar. Add cocoa mixture and vanilla, baking soda mixed with sour cream. Fold in flour and salt. Sift four times. Fold in egg whites.

Bake 20 to 30 minutes at 350° in greased and floured pans.

ICING: Melt milk, chocolate, sugar, syrup and butter on low heat. Turn up to high and when reaches rolling boil, cook one minute not stirring. Add 1 teaspoon vanilla and put pan in cold water until cool. Beat until thick.

Mrs. Joel Richardson (Ingrid)

AUNT BESS' JAPANESE FRUIT CAKE
100 year old recipe

Oven: 350° 20 min.—yellow layers
    30 min—spice layers   Yield: 14 to 16 servings

Cake:

1 cup butter
2 cups sugar
4 eggs
3 cups flour
1 tablespoon baking powder
    (heaping)
1 cup sweet milk

2 teaspoons vanilla
1 teaspoon powdered
    cinnamon
1 teaspoon cloves
1 teaspoon allspice
3/4 pound seedless raisins
    (cut fine)

Filling:

1 orange (rind and juice)
1 lemon (rind and juice)
Meat of one fresh coconut,
    grated fine

2 cups sugar
1 cup boiling water
2 tablespoons cornstarch

Cake: Cream butter with sugar. Add eggs and mix well. Sift flour 3 times with baking powder. Add alternately with sweet milk and vanilla. Mix well and bake 2 layers (9 inch pans).

Then add to remaining half of batter; cinnamon, cloves, and allspice. Add seedless raisins. Bake this in 2 layers.

Filling: Cook together rind and juice of orange, lemon, meat of fresh coconut grated fine, sugar, and boiling water. When this begins to boil, add cornstarch moistened in cold water. Cook until falls in heavy lump from spoon. Put between layers. Frost if desired.

                                    Mrs. Mitch Powell (Anne)

LEMON JELLO CAKE

Oven: 325° to 350° for 45 to 50 minutes   Yield: 1 tube cake

1 small box lemon Jello
1 cup hot water
1 box yellow or lemon
  supreme cake mix

3/4 cup oil
4 eggs
Dash of salt

Glaze:

juice of 2 lemons
1/2 cup sugar

grated rind of 1 lemon

Dissolve jello in hot water. Let cool. Add cake mix and oil alternately. Add eggs one at a time. Beat until smooth. Bake in greased and floured 10-inch tube pan at 325° to 350° for 45 to 50 minutes. Mix glaze ingredients and cook over medium heat until thickened. Pour over cake while cake is still warm.

Mrs. Sam Banks (Mary Willie)

PUNCH BOWL CAKE
Good for large group

Oven: As directed on package   Yield: 25 servings

1 yellow cake mix
2 small instant vanilla
  pudding
4 cups milk
1 can cherry pie filling

1 large can crushed pineapple,
  drained
3 bananas, sliced
1 large Cool Whip
1 cup chopped pecans

Bake cake mix by directions on box in 9x12 pan. Break in half and put half in bottom of punch bowl. Mix one package of vanilla pudding with 2 cups of milk and pour over cake. Top with half of the cherry pie filling, half of the bananas, half of pineapple, half of Cool Whip, and half of pecans. Put other half of cake in punch bowl and repeat process. If desired, decorate top with cherries.

Mrs. John D. Jones (Joanne)
Talbotton, Georgia

PRUNE CAKE

Oven: 325° for 50 minutes

3 eggs beaten
1 cup vegetable oil
1 1/2 cups sugar
1 cup buttermilk
1 1/2 teaspoons baking soda
2 cups plain flour
1 teaspoon cinnamon

1 teaspoon nutmeg
1 teaspoon allspice
1 teaspoon vanilla flavoring
1 cup cooked prunes (pitted and chopped)
1 cup chopped pecans

Mix together eggs, oil, sugar, buttermilk (in which soda is dissolved), flour, cinnamon, nutmeg, allspice and vanilla. Mix well. Add prunes and nuts, mixing well. Pour into 9x13″ baking dish and bake at 325° for 50 minutes.

TOPPING:

1 cup sugar
1/2 cup buttermilk
1/2 teaspoon baking soda

1 tablespoon White syrup
3/4 stick butter
1/2 teaspoon vanilla flavoring

Dissolve soda in buttermilk. Mix all ingredients and boil about one minute. Pour over the cake while it is still hot. (For a more moist cake, make tiny holes using fork in the cake so the topping can seep through.)

Jane Johnson
Fayetteville, Georgia

"Cooking is like love. It should be entered into with abandon or not at all."

Harriet Van Horne

STRAWBERRY CAKE
Easy—pretty in heart-shaped pan for Valentine's

Oven: 350° 25 to 30 minutes   Yield: 1 cake

1 box white cake mix
4 eggs
1 cup vegetable oil
1/2 cup hot water

1 small box strawberry Jello
1/2 (10 ounce) package
  strawberries

Mix cake mix, eggs and oil together. Melt Jello in hot water and add to cake mixture with strawberries. Bake at 350° for 25 to 30 minutes.

ICING:
1 box powdered sugar
1/2 (10 ounce) package
  strawberries

1 stick butter or margarine,
  room temperature

Mix together and spread on cooled cake.

Mrs. Duke Blackburn, Jr. (Lynn)

CLOUD CAKE
Quick and easy

Yield: 8-10 servings

1 angel food cake
1 (20 ounce) can crushed
  pineapple, drained

1 (4 ounce) Jello instant
  pudding
1 (8 ounce) Cool Whip

Cut cake into 3 layers. Combine remaining ingredients, mixing well. Spread mixture of filling on top of each layer. Stack layers and spread filling on sides. Refrigerate or freeze.

Mary Hall

209

PATIENCE COCONUT CAKE

Oven: According to package
Yield: 8-10 servings

CAKE:

16 ounces sour cream
16 ounces frozen coconut
2 cups powdered sugar

1 Betty Crocker yellow butter
cake mix

ICING:

1 large Cool Whip
16 ounce frozen coconut

CAKE: Mix sour cream, frozen coconut and powdered sugar and put into the refrigerator for 24 hours. Mix and bake the yellow butter cake according to package directions. Bake in two layer pans and when layers are cool, split in half. Spread sour cream mixture between the layers.

ICING: Combine the Cool Whip and coconut and ice the cake. Place the cake in a covered container and put in the refrigerator for 5 days before serving.

Mrs. Lonnie Lonergan, II (Ginny)

And Tom said, "Let us also take
An apple and a slice of cake;
which was enough for Tom and me
to go a-sailing on, till tea.

Robert Louis Stevenson

KENTUCKY BUTTER CAKE

Oven: 350° 60 to 65 minutes

3 cups flour	2 cups sugar
1 teaspoon baking powder	4 eggs
1 teaspoon salt	1 cup buttermilk
1/2 teaspoon soda	2 teaspoons vanilla
1 cup butter	

Butter Sauce:

1 cup sugar	1/2 cup butter
1/4 cup water	1 tablespoon vanilla

Sift together flour, baking powder, salt, and soda. Set aside. Cream butter and sugar. Blend in eggs one at a time, blending well after each. Combine buttermilk and vanilla and add alternately with dry ingredients to creamed mixture. Begin and end with dry ingredients. Blend well after each addition. Turn into 10-inch tube pan that has been greased on the bottom. Bake at 350° for 60 to 65 minutes. Run spatula along edge and stem of pan and prick cake with a fork. Pour hot sauce over cake. Cool before removing from pan. Sprinkle with powdered sugar just before serving.

Butter Sauce: Combine sugar, water and butter in a saucepan. Heat until butter is melted; DO NOT BOIL. Add vanilla.

Mrs. Carol Gruenert
Atlanta, Georgia

"Tis an ill cook that cannot lick his own fingers."
Shakespeare

COCA COLA CAKE

Do not over bake this cake. It is better after it sits for a day.
Cover tightly with foil to keep moist.

Oven: 350° 30 to 45 minutes   Yield: 15 servings

2 cups plain flour   1/2 cup buttermilk
2 cups sugar   2 eggs
1 1/2 sticks margarine   1 teaspoon baking soda
3 tablespoons cocoa   1 teaspoon vanilla
1 cup Coca Cola

Frosting:

2/3 cup margarine   1 (16 ounce) box powdered
6 tablespoons Coca Cola   sugar
3 tablespoons cocoa

Mix flour and sugar in bowl. In a saucepan, bring to boil margarine, cocoa, and Coca Cola. Pour over flour mixture. In separate bowl, beat buttermilk, eggs, baking soda, and vanilla and add to flour mixture. Pour into a 10x13 greased pan. Bake at 350° for 30 to 45 minutes.

While cake is baking, bring to boil margarine, Coca Cola and cocoa. Beat in powdered sugar. Pour onto cake while still in pan. Frosting will harden on cake as it cools.

Mrs. Frank Marchman (Beth Candler)

There is nothing better for a man, than that he should eat and drink and that he should make his soul enjoy in his labor.

Ecclesiastes 11:24

LUCY'S OATMEAL CAKE
Flavor enhanced if made a day ahead

Oven: 350° 30 to 40 minutes   Yield: 12 servings

1 1/2 cups boiling water   1 1/3 cups flour
1 cup oats   1 teaspoon soda
1/2 cup butter, softened   1/2 teaspoon salt
1 cup white sugar   1 1/2 teaspoons cinnamon
1 cup brown sugar   2 teaspoons vanilla
2 eggs, beaten   1/2 cup pecans, chopped

Topping:

6 tablespoons butter, melted   1/2 teaspoon vanilla
1/2 cup brown sugar   1/2 cup coconut
1/2 cup canned milk   1/2 cup pecans, chopped

Pour boiling water over oats and set aside. Cream butter, white sugar, brown sugar and eggs. Add oats. Sift together flour, soda, salt, and cinnamon. Mix into oat mixture and add vanilla and nuts. Bake at 350° for 30 to 40 minutes in 9x13 pan.

While cake is baking, combine topping ingredients in a saucepan and bring to a slight boil. Keep warm until cake has baked and spread on top of cake.

Mrs. Joe Distel (Pat)

A small house is more easily kept clean than a palace; taste may be quite as well displayed in the arrangement of dishes on a pine table as in grouping the silver and china of the rich.

The Dixie Cook-Book (1888)

LOVE LIGHT CHIFFON CAKE

Oven: 350° 30 minutes   Yield: 10 servings

2 eggs, separated
1 1/2 cups sugar
1 3/4 cup plain all-purpose
  flour
1/4 cup cocoa

3/4 teaspoon soda
1/4 teaspoon salt
1/3 cup oil plus 1 tablespoon
1 cup buttermilk

Beat egg whites with 1/2 cup sugar until stiff. Set aside. In large bowl, mix flour, sugar, cocoa, soda, salt, oil and 1/2 cup buttermilk. Beat 2 minutes. Add egg yolks and 1/2 cup buttermilk. Beat 2 minutes. Fold in egg whites. Pour into 3 (9-inch) pans. Bake 30 minutes at 350°.

Icing:

2 cups sugar
1 stick margarine
1/2 cup regular milk

1/4 cup cocoa
Dash of salt

Cook all ingredients 2 minutes after coming to a rapid boil. Set pan in cold water and beat until firm. Quickly ice the cake.

Mrs. Joseph C. Storey (Leona)

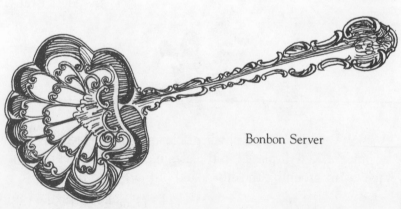

Bonbon Server

RED VELVET CAKE

Oven: 350° 30 to 35 minutes   Yield: 1 cake

1 1/2 cups oil	1 teaspoon salt
1 1/2 cups sugar	1 cup buttermilk
2 eggs	1 teaspoon soda
1 tablespoon cocoa	1 tablespoon vinegar
Red food coloring	1 teaspoon vanilla
2 1/4 cups plain flour	

CREAM CHEESE FROSTING:

1 box powdered sugar	1 stick butter or margarine,
1 (8 ounce) cream cheese,	room temperature
softened	1 cup nuts

Combine oil and sugar. Add eggs, one at a time, beating after each. Add cocoa and food coloring. Sift flour and salt together. Add alternately with buttermilk to cream mixture. Sprinkle soda and then vinegar over batter and stir until well blended. Add vanilla and pour in 2 cake pans. Bake at 350° for 30 to 35 minutes. Mix frosting ingredients together and spread on cool cake.

N. Marshall Cawthon

AMALGAMATION FILLING
Family recipe over 100 years old

8 egg yolks	1 cup chopped nuts
2 cups sugar	1 cup chopped raisins
1 cup butter	1 cup flaked coconut
1/4 cup orange juice	

Beat egg yolks. Add sugar, butter and orange juice. Cook over low heat until thick, stirring constantly with wooden spoon. Remove from heat and beat until it gets creamy. Add nuts, raisins and coconut. Spread filling between 3 layers of your favorite cake.

Martha Moultrie

CITY CAFÉ CHOCOLATE MOUSSE CAKE

Oven: 350° for 5 to 7 minutes   Yield: Approximately 10

Crust:

1 (14 ounce) package
    chocolate cookies, crushed

1/2 stick margarine, at room
    temperature
1 tablespoon sugar

Filling:

1/2 pint whipping cream
11 ounces semi-sweet
    chocolate (2 ounces
    shaved)
5 eggs, separated

1 ounce grand marnier
    liqueur
1 1/2 sticks unsalted butter
    (cut into cubes)
1 1/2 teaspoons water
1 pinch cream of tartar

Mix crust in a food processor. Press into springform pan and bake at 350° for 5 to 7 minutes. Remove from oven and refrigerate.

Whip egg whites with cream of tartar until stiff peaks form. Set aside.

Melt 9 ounces of the chocolate with the grand marnier and 1/2 teaspoon of water over low heat, keeping it smooth with rubber spatula. If it begins to crumble, add more water. After it becomes smooth and uniform, remove from heat and add butter 1 cube at a time until smooth.

Transfer contents to mixer bowl and begin adding egg yolks, 1 at a time, beating at medium speed. Mousse will begin to thicken. Turn speed down to low and spoon in the egg whites a little bit at a time until a marble texture is uniform.

Pour into crust and refrigerate for at least two hours.

Top with whipped cream and shaved chocolate.

Jack Deyton
City Café

TRADITIONAL SOUTHERN AMBROSIA

Yield: 6 servings

6 oranges
2 cups fresh grated coconut
(or bagged can be used)
1/2 cup sugar

1/3 cup sherry (or 1/4 cup
apricot brandy), optional
1 ripe pineapple, optional

Peel oranges and cut into sections. Place in layers in a bowl with each layer covered with sugar and coconut. Chill for several hours. If desired, you may pour sherry or apricot brandy over mixture. Also, a layer of thinly sliced pineapple slices may be layered with orange slices.

Mrs. Frank Marchman (Beth Candler)

EASY AMBROSIA

Yield: 8 servings

2 bananas
3 apples, peeled
1 small can flaked coconut
1 large can crushed pineapple
and juice

1 can water
1 (6 ounce) can concentrated
orange juice

Chop bananas rather fine. Prepare apples in food processor or chop fine. Mix all ingredients well. Chill.

Note: Can leave one apple unpeeled for color.

Martha W. Stukes

"Feast and your halls are crowded; Fast, and the world goes by."

Ella Wheeler Wilcox

217

PUMPKIN AND CREAM CHEESE ROLL-UP

Excellent Thanksgiving and Christmas dessert. Also makes a good
Bridge Club dessert. Pretty sliced on a party tray.

Oven: 375° 15 minutes   Yield: 10 servings

3/4 cup sifted all-purpose
  flour
1 teaspoon baking powder
2 teaspoons ground cinnamon
1 teaspoon pumpkin pie spice
1/2 teaspoon ground nutmeg

1/2 teaspoon salt
3 eggs, slightly beaten
1 cup sugar
2/3 cup canned solid-pack
  pumpkin
1 cup chopped walnuts

Cream Cheese Filling:

1 cup sifted 10-X sugar
1 (8 ounce) package cream
  cheese, softened

6 tablespoons buter
1 teaspoon vanilla

Pre-heat oven to 375°. Grease a 15x10x1 inch jelly roll pan.
Line with wax paper; grease and flour the wax paper. Sift flour,
baking powder, cinnamon, pumpkin pie spice, nutmeg and salt onto
wax paper. Beat eggs and sugar in large bowl until thick and fluffy;
beat in pumpkin.

Stir in sifted dry ingredients all at once. Pour into prepared
pan, spreading evenly with rubber spatula. Sprinkle with nuts. Bake
until center springs back when lightly touched with fingertips, about
15 minutes. Loosen cake around edges with a knife. Invert onto
clean, damp towel dusted with 10X sugar; peel off wax paper. Trim
1/4″ from all sides. Roll up cake and towel together from short side.
Place seam side down on wire rack; cool completely. Unroll cake.
Spread with cream cheese filling. Re-roll cake. Refrigerate until
ready to serve. Slice.

To make cream cheese filling beat together sugar, cream
cheese, butter and vanilla until smooth.

Mrs. Eugene Craven (Pat)

LEMON ORANGE DROPS
Makes over 100 cakes. Great for receptions.

Oven: 300° 10 to 15 minutes   Yield: 100 cakes

1 box lemon cake mix   1 1/2 cups water less 1
2 eggs   teaspoon

Icing:

1 1/2 pound confectioners'   Juice of 2 oranges
    sugar (sifted)   Grated rind from 1 lemon
Juice of 2 lemons   and 1 orange

Make icing first and set aside. Combine cake mix, eggs, and water. Use one level teaspoon of batter and place in greased and floured small muffin tins. Bake at 300° 10 to 15 minutes. Dunk hot cakes in icing. Drain on wax paper then move to another piece of wax paper. Let dry over night.

Mrs. William G. Scruggs (Barbara)

MEXICAN APPLE CRISP
Serve warm with whipped cream or ice cream

Oven: 350° 20 to 30 minutes   Yield: 6-8 servings

2 packages frozen (or 6 fresh   1 stick butter
    large) apples   1 (7 ounce) package
1 cup water   cinnamon tortilla chips (or
1/2 cup sugar   unsalted tortilla chips
1/4 cup raisins (optional)   sprinkled generously with
Pinch of salt   sugar and cinnamon)

Cook apples, water, and sugar in a saucepan until boiling. Add raisins and salt. Pour into 8x11" casserole dish. Cover with tortilla chips and mix in lightly. Sprinkle top with chips and dot with pats of butter. Bake at 350° for 20 to 30 minutes.

Mrs. Charles Craft (Madeline)

FRUIT PIZZA

Oven: 300° for 10 to 15 minutes   Yield: 8 servings

1/2 cup powdered sugar	1 cup sugar
3/4 cup cold butter or margarine	1 teaspoon vanilla
	Fresh fruit
1 1/2 cups flour	1 tablespoon cornstarch
1 (8 ounce) cream cheese, room temperature	1 cup fruit juice
	1 teaspoon lemon juice

Mix powdered sugar, butter and flour together to make a dough. Pat into pizza pan and bake at 300° for 10 to 15 minutes, until edges turn brown. Cool completely. Mix cream cheese, 1/2 cup sugar and vanilla together and spread on crust. Arrange fruit on cream cheese. (Use any fresh fruit—apples, oranges, bananas, kiwi fruit, grapes, strawberries, pineapple, peaches, pears, or substitute drained fruit cocktail.) Mix cornstarch, fruit juice, 1/2 cup sugar and lemon juice in saucepan. Heat until it boils and thickens. When cool, pour over fruit and refrigerate.

Mrs. David Kinrade (Joan)

EASY COBBLER CRUST
Especially good with peaches, blackberries, blueberries, or strawberries

Oven: 375° 30 to 45 minutes   Yield: 6-8 servings

1 quart fresh or frozen fruit with juices (sweetened to taste)	1/2 cup self-rising flour
	1/2 cup sugar
	1/2 cup buttermilk
1/2 stick butter	

Melt butter in 2-quart baking dish. Mix flour, sugar and buttermilk well. Pour mixture onto sizzling butter. Pour fruit mixture onto batter. Bake approximately 30 to 45 minutes until crust rises and is dark golden brown. Allow to stand at least 15 minutes before serving. Can be served with ice cream, milk, or cream.

Beverly Cotton

CHOCOLATE DELIGHT

Oven: 350° 20 to 25 minutes   Yield: 16 servings

1 cup plain flour
1/2 cup margarine (room
  temperature)
1 cup chopped pecans
1 (12 ounce) carton cool
  whip
1 cup powdered sugar, sifted

1 (8 ounce) package cream
  cheese
3 cups milk
1 package vanilla instant
  pudding
1 package chocolate instant
  pudding

Mix flour, margarine and pecans and press into a 9x13 dish or cake pan. Bake at 350° for 20 to 25 minutes. Cool. This makes crust.

Mix 1 cup cool whip, powdered sugar and cream cheese and spread over crust.

Mix both puddings with the 3 cups of milk and beat until slightly thickened. Spread over cream cheese layer. Top with rest of cool whip. Chill for several hours before serving. Cut into squares and top with a cherry or chopped pecans.

Mrs. John D. Jones (Joanne)
Talbotton, Georgia

"I'm tired of eatin cabbiges," say Brer Rabbit one mawnin! "An I'm tired of carrots, sparrer-grass an beans. I'd like ter sink my teef in somethin' sweet."

Joel Chandler Harris

221

TOFFEE ICE BOX DESSERT

1 cup butter
2 cups powdered sugar
3 egg yolks
2 ounces bitter chocolate, melted
1 teaspoon vanilla
3 egg whites

1/2 cup cream, (whip until very stiff)
1 cup blanched almonds, slivered and toasted (optional)
1/2 pound vanilla wafers

Cream butter. Gradually beat in sugar. Add egg yolks one at a time; beating well after each addition. Add melted chocolate and vanilla. Fold in stiffly beaten egg whites and whipped cream.

Roll vanilla wafers to a fine crumb and spread half in a buttered 10x10 inch pan. Spoon chocolate mixture over the vanilla wafer crums. Mix almonds with remaining crumbs and spread on top. Refrigerate overnight. Cut in squares and serve with whipped cream and top with a cherry.

Mrs. Mayo H. Royal, Sr. (Elizabeth)

BANANA PUDDING

Yield: 8 to 10 servings

1 large box vanilla pudding (instant)
3 cups milk
1 (8 ounce) container Cool Whip

1 can Eagle Brand milk
4 or 5 bananas
1 box vanilla wafers

Mix instant pudding with milk. Add Cool Whip and Eagle Brand milk. Layer bananas, wafers, and pudding mixture in a 3 quart flat Pyrex casserole dish. Save a few vanilla wafers and crush for sprinkling on top.

Note: Pudding is better the second day.

Mrs. William H. Banks (Betty)
Turin, Georgia

EVA MAE'S RICE PUDDING

Oven: Preheat to 400°   Yield: Serves 10

1 cup raw rice	3/4 cup sugar
3 large eggs, separated	1 1/2 teaspoon lemon extract
1 stick margarine	1 (6 ounce) frozen coconut

Rinse rice and cook in water for 20 minutes or until done. Separate eggs and beat yellows well and mix in rice and beat well. Add margarine, sugar, extract and coconut—let cool to get correct consistency. If needed, add a little milk. Beat egg whites, add 6 tablespoons of sugar. Egg whites should be stiff before spreading on pudding. Brown approximately 4 minutes.

Mrs. Curtis Tolbert (Eva Mae)

BUCKHEAD DINER PEACH BREAD PUDDING

1 pound brioche, sliced into 1/2" thick slices	6 eggs
	6 ounces sugar
3 ounces butter	1 1/2 pint milk
1 pound poached peaches, sliced	1 teaspoon cinnamon
	1 cup sugar
1 pound poached peaches, pureed (reserved 1 pt.)	1 quart heavy cream
	1/2 cup sugar

Lightly butter brioche slices and bake in oven until lightly toasted. Combine sliced peaches and puree and mix well. Combine eggs, sugar and milk and whisk vigorously for two minutes. Add peach puree and slices. Mix well. Generously butter 3" deep pan and dust with granulated sugar. Put down a layer of brioche toast and cover with peach custard mixture. Repeat until pan is 1/2" from top. Allow to stand for one hour. Sprinkle with cinnamon sugar. Cover with aluminum foil and bake at 275° for 1 hour and 15 minutes. Allow to rest for 2 hours. Cut into desired serving size and serve with peach puree and lightly sweetened soft whipped cream.

Gerry Klaskala
Buckhead Diner
Atlanta, GA

223

STRAWBERRY SHORTCAKE

Oven: 450° 15 to 18 miunutes   Yield: 6 to 8 servings

2 cups plain flour
2 tablespoons sugar
1 tablespoon baking powder
1/2 teaspoon salt

1/2 cup butter or margarine
1 egg, beaten
2/3 cup light cream

Topping:

Butter or margarine, softened
1 cup whipping cream

3 to 4 cups halved
   strawberries, sweetened
   with brown sugar

In mixing bowl, stir together flour, sugar, baking powder and salt. Cut in butter until mixture resembles coarse crumbs. Combine the egg and light cream and add all at once to flour mixture, stirring with fork just to moisten. Spread dough in greased 8x1 1/2-inch round baking pan, building up edges slightly. Bake in a 450° oven for 15 to 18 minutes or until done. Remove from pan and cool slightly. During baking, whip cream in a chilled bowl to form soft peaks (tips curl over). Using a sharp knife, gently split shortcake, horizontally, into two layers. Lift off top carefully. Place bottom layer on serving plate. Spread a little softened butter over bottom layer. Spoon one-half of the strawberries and whipped cream over layer. Top with second layer. Spoon remaining strawberries and whipped cream over top. Serve while cake is warm.

Margaret Anne Watkins
Atlanta, Georgia

"It's certain that fine women eat
A crazy salad with their meat
Whereby the Thorn of Plenty is undone."

William Butler Yeats

PUMPKIN CHEESE CAKE

Oven: 325° 1 hour 15 minutes   Yield: 10 servings

1 1/2 cups graham cracker crumbs

1/2 stick (1/4 cup) butter or margarine, melted

1 3/4 teaspoons ground ginger

3 packages (8 ounces) cream cheese, softened

1 can (14 ounces) sweetened condensed milk

1 can (1 pound) pumpkin

3 extra large eggs

1 1/2 teaspoons cinnamon

1 teaspoon nutmeg

1/2 teaspoon salt

Sweetened whipped cream

Combine crumbs, margarine and 3/4 teaspoon of the ginger. Press firmly on bottom of a 9-inch spring form pan. In large mixer bowl, beat cheese until fluffy. Gradually beat in sweetened condensed milk until smooth. Add remaining 1 teaspoon ginger, pumpkin, eggs, cinnamon, nutmeg and salt. Mix well. Pour over crumb crust in pan. Bake in preheated 325° oven about 1 hour and 15 minutes or until cracks start to appear around edge and cake springs back when lightly touched. Center will be slightly soft but will get firm as cake cools. Cool cake to room temperature. Refrigerate until thoroughly chilled. Serve with whipped cream.

Mrs. Walter M. Lonergan II (Ginny)

The friendly cow all red and white,
I love with all my heart:
she gives me cream with all her might,
to eat with apple tart.

Robert Louis Stevenson

THE ULTIMATE CHEESECAKE

Oven: 400° 10 minutes
      250° 1 hour   Yield: 16 servings

Crust:

1 cup sifted all-purpose flour
  (sift before measuring)
1/4 cup sugar
1 teaspoon grated lemon peel

1/2 teaspoon vanilla extract
1 egg yolk
1/4 cup butter, softened

Pineapple glaze:

2 tablespoons sugar
4 teaspoons cornstarch
2 cans (8 1/2 ounce size)
  crushed pineapple in heavy
  syrup, undrained

2 tablespoons lemon juice
2 drops yellow food color

Filling:

5 packages (8 ounce size)
  cream cheese, softened
  (Hint: Put out about an
  hour before use)
1 3/4 cups sugar
3 tablespoons flour

2 teaspoons grated lemon peel
1 1/2 teaspoons grated orange
  peel
1/4 teaspoon vanilla extract
5 eggs, plus 2 egg yolks
1/4 cup heavy cream

Preheat oven to 400°. Grease inside of 9 inch springform pan (3 inches high). Remove side. Make crust: In medium bowl, combine flour, sugar, lemon peel, vanilla. Make well in center. With fork blend in yolk and butter. Mix with fingertips until smooth.

On bottom of pan, form half of dough into ball. Place waxed paper on top. Roll pastry to edge of pan. Remove paper. Bake 6 to 8 minutes or until golden. Cool. Meanwhile, divide rest of dough into three parts. Cut six strips of waxed paper, 3 inches wide.

On dampened surface, between paper strips, roll each part 2 1/4 inches wide and 9 inches long. Assemble springform pan with crust on bottom. Line inside of pan with pastry strips overlapping ends. Remove waxed paper strips. Preheat oven to 450.°

Filling: In large mixer bowl, blend cheese, sugar, flour, peels and vanilla at high speed. Beat in egg yolks, one at a time: beat until smooth, occasionally scraping bowl with spatula. Beat in cream. Pour into pan. Bake 10 minutes. Lower oven to 250°. Bake 1 hour longer. Remove to rack to cool—two hours.

Make glaze: In small saucepan, combine sugar and cornstarch. Stir in remaining ingredients. Over medium heat, bring to boiling, stirring; boil 1 minute or until thickened and translucent. Cool.

Spread surface of cheesecake with glaze; refrigerate until well chilled—three hours or overnight. To serve: Loosen pastry from side of pan with spatula. Remove side of springform pan. Garnish with sliced strawberries, if desired. Cut into wedges. Serves 16—at least.

Sarah Johnson

MOCHA CHOCOLATE CHIP CHEESECAKE

Oven: 200° 2 hours   Yield: 1 cheesecake

1 1/2 cups chocolate wafer
  crumbs (about 24 wafers)
6 tablespoons butter, softened
1/3 cup crushed pecans
1 1/2 pounds cream cheese,
  softened
1 cup sugar

4 eggs, room temperature
1/3 cup heavy cream
1 tablespoon instant coffee
1 1/2 teaspoons vanilla
1 cup miniature chocolate
  chips

Put rack in center of oven and preheat to 200°. Butter a 9 inch springform pan. Combine wafer crumbs, butter, and pecans in food processor and mix well. Pat onto bottom and sides of pan. Beat cream cheese with mixer until fluffy. Blend in sugar. Add eggs one at a time. Add cream, coffee, and vanilla and beat for 2 minutes. Pour into crust. Top with chocolate chips and swirl with spatula. Bake for two hours or longer, until set.

Mrs. William M. Berry, III (Anne Jarrell)

STRAWBERRY GLAZED CREAM CHEESE CAKE

Oven: 350° 40 to 45 minutes;
      then 5 minutes longer   Yield: 10-12 servings

CRUST

3/4 cup coarsely ground
  walnuts (3 ounces)
3/4 cup finely crushed graham
  crackers

3 tablespoons melted unsalted
  butter

Position rack in center of oven and preheat to 350°. Lightly butter a 10″ spring form pan.

Combine walnuts, graham cracker crumbs and butter. Press compactly onto bottom of prepared pan.

FILLING

4 (8 ounce) packages cream
  cheese, room temperature
4 eggs
1 1/4 cups sugar

1 tablespoon fresh lemon
  juice
1 tablespoon vanilla
1 teaspoon lemon extract

Beat cream cheese in large bowl of electric mixer until smooth. Add eggs, sugar, lemon juice, vanilla, and lemon extract and beat thoroughly. Spoon over crust.

Set pan on baking sheet to catch any batter that may drip out. Bake 40 to 45 minutes. (Cake may rise slightly and crack in several areas; it will settle again, cracks will minimize and topping will cover it up). Let stand at room temperature 15 minutes. Retain oven temperature at 350°.

TOPPING

1 1/2 cups sour cream   1 teaspoon vanilla
1/4 cup sugar (minus 1
   teaspoon)

Combine sour cream, sugar, vanilla, and blend well. Cover and refrigerate. When cake has finished baking, spoon topping over, starting at center and extending to within 1/2 inch of edge. Return to oven and bake 5 minutes longer. Allow to cool, then refrigerate cheesecake for *at least 24 hours, preferably, for 2 to 3 days.* Cake can be wrapped well in plastic wrap and frozen at this point. When ready to thaw, place in refrigerator overnight.

GLAZE

1 quart medium strawberries   1 tablespoon cornstarch
1 (12-ounce) jar red   1/4 cup cointreau
   raspberry jelly   1/4 cup water

Several hours before serving, wash and hull berries and let dry completely on paper towels. Combine a little jelly with cornstarch in saucepan and mix well. Add remaining jelly, cointreau, and water. Cook over medium heat, stirring frequently until thickened and clear, about 5 minutes. Cool to lukewarm, stirring occasionally. Using knife, loosen cake from pan, removing spring form. Dip berries in glaze and arrange berries, pointed end up over top of cake in a circular pattern. Spoon glaze over berries, allowing some to drip down side of cake. Return to refrigerator until glaze is firm.

Anne Walkins
Atlanta, Georgia

"When a man is invited to dinner, he is disappointed if he does not get something good."

Samuel Johnson

FROZEN CHOCOLATE SUNDAE

Yield: 18 to 20 servings

1 small can Pet milk
1 package (6 ounces)
  chocolate chips

1 (10 1/2 ounce) package
  miniature marshmallows
1/2 gallon vanilla ice cream

Melt above ingredients (*except* ice cream) in a double boiler. Cool.

Crumb Mixture:

1/2 cup melted oleo
1 1/3 cups coconut

2 cups graham cracker
  crumbs
1 cup pecans, chopped

Brown oleo and coconut slightly. Add graham cracker crumbs and pecans. Cool.

Place 3/4 crumb mixture in bottom of an oblong pan. Cut 1/2 gallon of vanilla ice cream into 1/2" slices. Cover crumbs with one layer of ice cream (using 1/2 of ice cream). Pour 1/2 of the chocolate mixture over this. Place rest of the ice cream over the above, then pour rest of chocolate over this layer. Sprinkle with remaining crumbs. Freeze.

Mrs. Harry Hunter (Margaret)

 ## SHERRY ICE CREAM

Yield: 1/2 gallon

3 egg yolks
1 cup sugar
Pinch of salt

2 cups milk
4 cups heavy whipping cream
1/3 cup sherry

Beat egg yolks together. Add sugar and salt. Heat milk. Pour egg mixture into hot milk, mixing well. Cook in double boiler until thick. Cook very slowly, stirring constantly—too much heat will curdle milk. Cool. Add whipping cream and sherry. Freeze in ice cream freezer.

Mrs. Frank Sheffield (Quenelle)
Americus, Georgia

GINGER ICE CREAM

Yield: 1/2 gallon

2 eggs
1 1/2 cups sugar
2 cups milk
1 cup ginger preserves (with syrup), finely cut

1 tablespoon chopped Maraschino cherries
4 tablespoons sherry
4 cups cream
1 teaspoon vanilla

Beat eggs together, adding 1/2 cup sugar while beating. Beat until light and thick. Heat milk on stove (or in microwave for 3 minutes on HIGH) and slowly pour into egg mixture, mixing well. Cook in a double boiler (or in microwave for 3 1/2 minutes on HIGH, whisking once a minute) until mixture is thick and coats the back of a spoon. Add ginger preserves, chopped cherries and sherry. Leave overnight in refrigerator. When ready to freeze, sweeten cream with 1 cup sugar and vanilla and add to mixture.

Mrs. William M. Berry, III (Anne Jarrell)

MAPLE-PECAN ICE CREAM
For 1-gallon churn freezer

1 1/2 quart half-and-half cream
1 pint of milk
1 cup whipping cream

1 1/4 cup maple syrup (or less, to taste)
2 whole eggs
1 cup coarsely chopped pecans

Blend first 5 ingredients quickly in blender. (Do not whip cream—use it as it comes from the carton). Heat in double boiler until thick and coats back of spoon.

Sauté pecans in 1 tablespoon butter. Chill. Set aside until later.

Freeze milk, cream, syrup and egg mixture in the crank freezer (or electric churn type freezer.) When ice cream is half frozen, add the cold chopped nuts. Finish turning until ice cream is frozen and will not turn any more. Pack well in ice and salt, after removing dasher. Eat in the next hour or so.

Dale and Nancy Sizemore
Moreland, GA

231

PEANUT BUTTER ICE CREAM

Yield: 1 gallon

2 cups sugar
6 eggs
2 pints cream (1 quart)
1 quart whole milk

1 1/2 cups chunky peanut butter
Vanilla

Combine sugar and eggs. Mix very well with electric mixer.

Combine cream with whole milk and chunky peanut butter in heavy saucepan. Cook over medium heat 5 to 10 minutes, stirring frequently. Add to egg mixture. Mix well and cook until thick. Add vanilla. Freeze in 1 gallon ice cream freezer.

Optional: Garnish with chocolate shavings or sprinkle with crushed oreo cookies (or add to custard mixture before freezing).

Mary Lynn Hall

ICE CREAM DESSERT

Oven: Bake cookies as directed on package   Yield: 12 servings

1 roll Pillsbury butterscotch or peanut butter cookies

1/2 gallon vanilla ice cream, softened

Sauce:

1 stick margarine
1 cup light brown sugar

1/2 cup evaporated milk
1 teaspoon vanilla flavoring

Bake cookies as directed on the package. After cooling, crumble cookies in bottom of a 9x13 inch dish. Spread softened ice cream over cookies. While cookies are baking and cooling, stir and boil sauce ingredients for 6 to 9 minutes until slightly thickened. Let cool. Sauce is to be poured over ice cream and spread evenly. Return to freezer for at least 1 hour before serving. (Dessert may be stored and served for 1 to 2 days.)

Mrs. Anne Arnold

IN CLOVER SUNDAE

Vanilla ice cream
Orange Brandy Sauce (recipe below)

Lace Cookies (In Clover Lace Cookies (see index)

Put a scoop of vanilla ice cream in each sundae dish. Spoon warm orange brandy sauce over ice cream and crumble a lace cookie over top. Serve immediately with lace cookies.

Orange Brandy Sauce:

8 ounces frozen orange juice concentrate
3/4 cup sugar
1/2 cup pineapple
4 1/2 cups water

Peel of one orange
6 ounces seedless raisins
4 tablespoons cornstarch
1 ounce brandy

In large saucepan mix together the orange juice, sugar, pineapple and 2 cups of water. Place on low heat. Meanwhile place 1/2 cup water and the orange peel in a blender and puree. Add the orange peel to the saucepan. Place 1 1/2 cups water in the blender with raisins and chop coarsely. Add the raisins to the saucepan. Blend the cornstarch into 1/2 cup water and add to mixture. Bring to a boil, stirring constantly. Add the brandy and serve hot. Sauce may be made ahead and reheated.

In Clover
LaGrange, Georgia

TROPICAL SHERBET

Yield: 1/2 gallon

Juice of 3 lemons
Juice of 3 oranges
3 ripe bananas, mashed well

3 cups sugar
7 cups lowfat milk

Mix ingredients well. Chill well before freezing in ice cream freezer. Serve with fresh mint garnish.

Mrs. William M. Berry, III (Anne Jarrell)

233

BASIC VANILLA ICE CREAM

2 (14-ounce) cans sweetened   1 tablespoon plus 1 teaspoon
   condensed milk   vanilla extract
1 quart half-and-half

Combine all ingredients, mixing well. Pour ice cream mixture into freezer can of a 1-gallon hand-turned or electric freezer. Freeze according to manufacturer's instructions. Ripen ice cream 1 hour, if desired. Yield: 2 1/2 quarts.

Rainbow Candy Ice Cream: Stir 1 1/2 cups candy-coated milk chocolate pieces into ice cream mixture just before freezing.

Coffee Ice Cream: Combine 2/3 cup hot water and 1 tablespoon instant coffee granules, stirring until granules dissolve. Let cool slightly. Stir coffee mixture into ice cream mixture just before freezing.

Mocha Ice Cream: Combine 1 cup hot water and 1 tablespoon instant coffee granules, stirring until granules dissolve. Let mixture cool slightly. Stir coffee mixture and 1 (5 1/2-ounce) can chocolate syrup (1/2 cup) into ice cream mixture just before freezing.

Toffee Ice Cream: Stir 1 (6-ounce) package toffee-flavored candy pieces into ice cream mixture just before freezing.

Mint-Chocolate Chip Ice Cream: Stir 1/2 cup green crème de menthe and 1 (6-ounce) package semisweet chocolate mini-morsels (1 cup) into ice cream mixture before freezing.

Buter Pecan Ice Cream: Add 1 tablespoon butter flavoring and 2 cups coarsely chopped toasted pecans to ice cream mixture just before freezing.

Lemonade Ice Cream: Add 1 (6-ounce) can frozen lemonade concentrate, thawed and undiluted, to ice cream mixture before freezing.

Cherry-Pecan Ice Cream: Substitute 1 teaspoon almond extract for vanilla, and add 1/3 cup maraschino cherry juice to ice cream mixture; freeze ice cream as directed. Stir 3/4 cup quartered maraschino cherries and 3/4 cup chopped pecans into ice cream after freezing.

Strawberry-Banana-Nut Ice Cream: Stir 3 bananas, mashed; 1 pint strawberries, coarsely chopped; and 3/4 cup chopped pecans into ice cream mixture just before freezing.

Peanut Butter Ice Cream: Stir 3/4 cup chunky peanut butter into ice cream mixture just before freezing. Serve ice cream with chocolate syrup, if desired.

Blueberry Ice Cream: Stir 2 cups fresh or frozen blueberries into ice cream mixture just before freezing.

Double-Chocolate Ice Cream: Stir 1 (5 1/2-ounce) can chocolate syrup (1/2 cup) and 1 (6-ounce) package semisweet chocolate mini-morsels (1 cup) into ice cream mixture just before freezing.

Black Forest Ice Cream: Stir 1 (5 1/2-ounce) can chocolate syrup (1/2 cup) and 1 (16 1/2 ounce) can pitted Bing cherries, drained and halved, into ice cream mixture just before freezing.

Chocolate-Covered Peanut Ice Cream: Stir (5 1/2 ounce) can chocolate syrup (1/2 cup) and 2 (7-ounce) packages chocolate-covered peanuts (2 cups) into ice cream mixture just before freezing.

Cookies and Cream Ice Cream: Break 15 cream-filled chocolate sandwich cookies into small pieces; stir into ice cream mixture just before freezing.

Maxine Pinson
Savannah, Georgia
Copyright by *Southern Living*;
reprinted by permission

"I have been sent to procure an angel to do cooking."

Emerson

235

BRANDY ALEXANDER
Great after a heavy meal!

Yields: 1 1/2 drinks

Breyers Vanilla Bean Ice Cream
B & B Liquor
Whipping cream (Half and Half may be substituted)

Cream de Cocoa
Nutmeg

Combine 2 scoops ice cream, 1 jigger of B & B (1 1/2 oz.), 1/2 cup whipping cream and 3/4 oz. Cream de Cocoa in blender and blend until frothy. Serve in champagne glass and top with grated nutmeg. This recipe should be adjusted to suit individual taste. Keep adding until you are happy. Use only the best quality ingredients. The secret is in the quality! B & B is better than Brandy and Breyers seems to add more body than other ice creams.

Mrs. Delia T. Crouch

Cafe Royale Spoon with Demitasse

GERMAN CHOCOLATE BROWNIES

Oven: 350° 40 to 45 minutes   Yield: 16 brownies

1 (4 ounce) package German
    Chocolate
2 tablespoons margarine
3 eggs
1 1/2 teaspoons vanilla
1 cup sugar
1/2 cup plain flour, not sifted

1/2 teaspoon baking powder
1/4 teaspoon salt
1/2 cup chopped pecans or
    walnuts
1 (3 ounce) package cream
    cheese, softened

Melt chocolate and margarine and cool. Beat 2 eggs with 1 teaspoon vanilla in bowl and add 3/4 cup sugar. Continue beating until thick. Sift flour, baking powder and salt together and add to egg mixture, mixing well. Blend in cooled chocolate mixture and nuts and set aside. Cream together cream cheese and 1/4 cup sugar until fluffy. Blend in 1 egg and 1/2 teaspoon vanilla. Spread half of chocolate mixture in greased and floured 8x8x2 inch pan. Pour cream cheese mixture over top. Drop spoonfuls of remaining chocolate mixture on cream cheese mixture. With small spatula, swirl through layers to marble. Bake in 350° oven for 40 to 45 minutes. Cut in squares when completely cooled.

Mrs. Don Tomlinson (Jane)
Asheville, North Carolina

Dessert party can include an after dinner coffee bar. Serve coffee with a variety of toppings and additives. For example: whipped cream, Kahlua, chocolate shavings, cinnamon, Amaretto, other liqueurs, honey, maple syrup, etc.

CHOCOLATE MINT BROWNIES

Oven: 350° 25 to 28 minutes   Yield: 36 bars

4 ounces unsweetened
  chocolate
1/2 pound margarine
4 eggs
Pinch of salt

1 teaspoon vanilla extract
2 cups granulated sugar
1 cup all-purpose flour, sifted
1 cup chopped pecans

Preheat oven to 350°. Melt the chocolate and margarine. Stir until smooth. With electric mixer beat the eggs until they are foamy. Beat in salt, vanilla, and sugar. Add the chocolate mixture and beat to mix. On low speed add the flour and beat only until mixed. Stir in the nuts. Pour into 13x9" greased and floured pan. Bake 25 to 28 minutes. Remove from oven and let stand at room temperature until cool.

MINT ICING

4 tablespoons margarine at
  room temperature
2 cups sifted powdered sugar

1 1/2 to 2 tablespoons milk
1 teaspoon peppermint extract
Few drops green food coloring

Beat until smooth with electric mixer. Spread evenly over the cake still in the pan. It will be a thin layer. Refrigerate 5 minutes before adding chocolate glaze.

CHOCOLATE GLAZE

1 package sweet German
  chocolate
4 tablespoons butter or
  margarine

1 teaspoon vanilla flavoring

Melt chocolate and butter. Add vanilla flavoring. Stir until smooth. Pour evenly over mint icing.

Refrigerate before cutting into small bars.

Mrs. Clark Hudson (Corille)

NOTE: These may be frozen and are especially good when served cold. They make a very pretty party or tea food when cut into tiny squares.

CHEESE CAKE SQUARES

Almond or vanilla flavoring can be added to the cream cheese layer.

Oven: 350° 35 minutes
Yield: 2 dozen

1 yellow cake mix
1 egg
1 stick margarine or butter, softened

1 (8 ounce) package cream cheese, softened
2 eggs
1 box powdered sugar
1/2 cup chopped nuts (rolled in powdered sugar)

Combine the first 3 ingredients with electric beater until evenly mixed. Press with a fork into a greased and floured 9x13" pan. Combine the next 3 ingredients with electric beater until smooth and pour over bottom layer. Top with nuts that have been tossed in confectioners' sugar. Bake at 350° for 35 minutes. Let cool then cut into squares. Store leftovers in refrigerator.

Mrs. Chip Goen (Sallie)

MINIATURE CHEESECAKES

Oven: 350° 15 to 20 minutes
Yield: about 24

4 (8 ounce) packages cream cheese
1 cup sugar
Pinch of salt

4 eggs, beaten well
2 teaspoons lemon juice
Graham cracker or vanilla wafer crumbs

Beat first five ingredients until smooth. After spraying small muffin tin with Pam, sprinkle with graham cracker crumbs or vanilla wafer crumbs. Fill cups about 3/4 full. Bake at 350° for 15 to 20 minutes. Can be served plain, with nuts, or covered with cherries. (Pie filling cherries preferred)

Florine Johnson

BUTTERSCOTCH CHEESECAKE SQUARES

Oven: 350° 25 to 30 minutes

Yield: 2 dozen

1 (12 ounce) package
  butterscotch morsels
1/3 cup margarine
2 cups graham cracker
  crumbs
1 cup chopped nuts

1 (8 ounce) package cream
  cheese, softened
1 (14 ounce) can Eagle Brand
  condensed milk
1 teaspoon vanilla
1 egg

Preheat oven to 350° (325° for glass dish). In medium saucepan melt morsels and margarine; stir in crumbs and nuts. Press half of mixture firmly onto bottom of greased 13x9″ baking pan. In large bowl, beat cheese until fluffy; beat in condensed milk, vanilla and egg. Mix well, pour into prepared pan; top with remaining crumb mixture. Bake 25 to 30 minutes or until toothpick inserted near center comes out clean. Cool to room temperature; chill before cutting into bars. Refrigerate leftovers.

Mrs. Chip Goen (Sallie)

HOMEMADE CHOCOLATE PEANUT BUTTER SQUARES

Yield: 24 bars

1 cup butter
2 cups smooth (or crunchy)
  peanut butter
1 1/4 cups graham cracker
  crumbs

1 (16-ounce) box powdered
  sugar
1 (6-ounce) package chocolate
  morsels

Melt butter and peanut butter. Add cracker crumbs and sugar. Mix well. Press into 13x9 inch pan. Melt chocolate morsels and spread over mixture. Cool and cut into squares.

Mrs. Don Tomlinson (Jane)
Asheville, North Carolina

PUMPKIN SQUARES
Best if eaten right away

Oven: 325° 45 minutes

Yield: 1-2 dozen

1 box yellow cake mix
1 stick margarine, melted
3 eggs
1 can pumpkin
1 cup sugar
1/2 small can evaporated milk

1 1/2 teaspoons cinnamon
1/2 teaspoon ginger
1/2 teaspoon salt
1/4 teaspoon mace
1/4 teaspoon nutmeg

Mix cake mix, oleo and 1 egg together. Reserve 1 cup for topping and spread rest in a 9x13″ Pyrex dish. Combine 2 eggs with remaining ingredients and pour over cake mixture. Crumble reserved topping mixture over pumpkin mixture and bake at 325° for 45 minutes. Serve warm with whipped cream.

Mrs. Larry Taylor (Barbara)

OLD FASHIONED GINGERBREAD

Oven: 350° 35 minutes

Yield: 12 servings

1/2 cup boiling water
1/2 cup shortening
1/2 cup brown sugar
1/2 cup molasses
1 egg, beaten
1 1/2 cups flour

1/2 teaspoon salt
1/2 teaspoon baking powder
1/2 teaspoon baking soda
1/4 teaspoon ginger
3/4 teaspoon cinnamon

Pour water over shortening. Add sugar, molasses, and egg. Beat well. Sift remaining dry ingredients and add to wet mixture. Beat until smooth. Bake in waxed paper lined, 8-inch square pan at 350° for 35 minutes. Cool in pan.

Mrs. Sam Candler (Betsy)
Sharpsburg, Georgia

LEMON SQUARES

Oven: 350° 45 minutes   Yield: 15 servings

CRUST:

1 cup unsifted all-purpose
  flour
2 tablespoons granulated
  sugar

1/8 teaspoon salt
1/3 cup soft butter

GLAZE:

1 tablespoon lemon juice
2/3 cup powdered sugar

1 teaspoon lemon rind, grated

MIXTURE:

2 beaten eggs
1/2 cup chopped pecans
1 cup firmly packed light
  brown sugar
1 cup flaked coconut

1 teaspoon vanilla
1/8 teaspoon baking powder
1 tablespoon lemon juice
1 teaspoon grated lemon rind

Mix all crust ingredients together until it resembles coarse meal and press in ungreased 9x13″ pan. Bake at 350° for 15 minutes. Mix all "mixture" ingredients together and spread over baked crust. Bake 30 minutes longer. Loosen edges, spread on lemon glaze and cool. Cut into small squares.

Mrs. Dennis McEntire (Sally)

An undisputed queen am I my realm I proudly rule,
A rolling pin's my scepter and my throne's a kitchen stool.

Betty Heisser

TRIPLE LAYER DELIGHTS

Yield: 36 squares

First Layer:

1/2 cup butter	1 egg slightly beaten
1/4 cup sugar	2 cups graham cracker
1/4 cup cocoa	crumbs
1 teaspoon vanilla	1 cup flaked coconut

Combine butter, sugar, cocoa and vanilla in the top of a double boiler. Stir until butter melts and then stir in egg until the mixture thickens (about 1 to 2 minutes). Then add graham cracker crumbs and coconut. Pour mixture into a buttered 9 inch square pan and press it evenly in pan.

Second Layer:

1/2 cup butter	2 cups sifted powdered sugar
3 tablespoons milk	
1 (3 1/2 ounce) package	
instant vanilla pudding	

Beat butter well and add all ingredients and beat mixture until it is fluffy. Spread over first layer and chill until it is firm.

Third Layer:

1 (6 ounce) package	2 tablespoons butter
semisweet chocolate chips	

Melt chocolate chips and butter in a double boiler and stir. Spread over chilled first and second layer and chill until hard. Cut into small bite-sized bars and keep in the refrigerator.

Mrs. Walter M. Lonergan II (Ginny)

CHEWY BARS

Oven: 250° 15 minutes / 325° 30 minutes   Yield: 32 brownies

2 cups toasted pecans
1 stick margarine
1 box (16 ounce) light brown
  sugar (use all but 1/2 cup)

3 eggs
2 cups self-rising flour, sifted
1 teaspoon vanilla

Toast pecans in a 250° oven for 15 minutes. In a double boiler melt margarine. Add brown sugar and add eggs that have been beaten. Stir constantly, cooking until the mixture is syrupy. Remove from heat and cool until lukewarm.

Put this mixture in a mixing bowl, adding sifted flour. Mix well. Add vanilla and toasted pecans. Bake in a 13x9" greased and floured pan at 325° for about 30 minutes. Cut into squares (approximately 32) after cooling. Very chewy!

Variation: add 12 ounce package chocolate chips.

Jimmie Shell
Turin, Georgia

CHEWY CARAMEL BARS

Oven: 350° 30 minutes   Yield: 18 servings

64 caramels
10 tablespoons milk
1 1/2 cups brown sugar
2 cups flour
1 teaspoon soda
1/2 teaspoon salt

2 cups quick cooking oats
3 sticks margarine, softened
12 ounce bag chocolate chips
6 ounce bag butterscotch
  chips

In saucepan, melt caramels in milk over low heat, cool slightly. Cream together margarine and brown sugar, then add other dry ingredients. Put half of the mixture into the bottoms of two 9" square pans. Bake 10 minutes at 350°. Remove from oven and sprinkle with chocolate and butterscotch chips. Drizzle caramel mixture over top. Top with remaining half of creamed mixture. Bake 20 minutes at 350°. Cool completely before cutting.

Mrs. Donald Sprayberry (Terri)

TURTLE BARS
Very rich

Oven: 350° 18 to 22 minutes   Yield: 3 to 4 dozen bars

CRUST:
2 cups plain flour
1 cup brown sugar

1/2 cup real butter (1 stick)

CARAMEL LAYER:
2/3 cup real butter
1 cup whole pecan halves

1/2 cup brown sugar
1 cup milk chocolate chips

Combine crust ingredients and pat firmly into ungreased 9x13x2 inch pan. Sprinkle pecans over crust. In heavy saucepan, combine brown sugar and butter. Cook and stir constantly until entire surface begins to boil. Boil 1/2 to 1 minute, then remove. Pour evenly over crust and pecans. Bake at 350° for 18 to 22 minutes, until bubbly and golden brown. Sprinkle with chocolate chips and allow to melt. (Swirl melted chips for marbled effect.) Cool completely, then cut into bars.

Mrs. Don Tomlinson (Jane)
Asheville, North Carolina

MUESLI BARS

Oven: 350°   Yield: 20 bars

1/2 cup unsalted butter, softened
1/3 cup firmly packed brown sugar
3 tablespoons honey

1 cup quick-cooking oats (uncooked)
1/3 cup almonds or hazelnuts
1/3 cup shredded coconut
1/3 cup sesame seeds

In a medium sauce pan over low heat, combine butter, brown sugar and honey. Cook until butter is melted and sugar is dissolved. Remove from heat. Add oats, nuts, coconut and sesame seeds. Press mixture evenly into a greased 11x7x2 pan. Bake at 350° for 15 to 18 minutes (or until golden brown). Let cool 15 minutes. Score into bars, then let cool completely. Cut into bars and remove from pan.

OPTION: Dip bars into melted chocolate.

Mrs. David Cotton (Pat)

BOURBON BARS

Oven: 350° 30 minutes
  300° until toasted
Yield: 15 bars

4 eggs
1 cup sugar
2 teaspoons vanilla
2 tablespoons bourbon
1 cup oil

3 cups flour
1 cup chopped nuts
1 teaspoon baking powder
Pinch salt

Beat first four ingredients together. Add 1 cup of oil and beat into mixture. Fold in flour, nuts, baking powder and salt. Bake in 350° oven for 30 minutes, in an ungreased pan (10x15″). Cut when warm. Toast in 300° oven until brown on one side. Turn over and toast on the other side like Zweiback.

This is a tried and true recipe that has been handed down from one generation to the next—so enjoy! Try to eat just one!

Mrs. Billy Abraham (Helen)

WHISKEY RINGS

Oven: 400° 10 minutes
Yield: 5 to 6 dozen cookies

1 pound of butter
6 hard boiled egg yolks
4 cups of flour

1/2 cup of sugar
1/2 wine glass of whiskey
  (2 1/2 to 3 oz.)

Mash all hard boiled egg yolks very fine. Mix all of the ingredients together. Roll very thin and cut with a doughnut or cookie cutter. Bake until light brown in a quick oven of 400° for about 10 minutes. Sprinkle with sugar while hot. Handle carefully, very brittle.

Melba G. Meyer
Stone Mountain, Georgia

MARGARET FRALEY'S PEANUT BUTTER COOKIES

Oven: 375° 10 minutes   Yield: 4 to 5 dozen

1/2 cup shortening
1/2 cup butter, soften
1 cup white sugar
1 cup brown sugar
1 cup peanut butter

2 eggs, beaten
3 cups flour
1 teaspoon soda
1/2 teaspoon salt
1 teaspoon vanilla

Cream shortening and butter. Add sugar and mix. Add peanut butter and eggs, mix well. Add dry ingredients, mix well. Add vanilla.

Shape with hands in ball, size of a large marble. Place an inch apart on buttered cookie sheet. Press 2 ways with fork to flatten and mark. Bake in 375° oven about 10 minutes or until golden brown. Cool. Set on paper towels before storing. Great fun for the kids!

Mrs. Joe Distel (Pat)

PEANUT BLOSSOMS

Oven: 375° 10 to 12 minutes   Yield: 48 cookies

1 3/4 cups all purpose flour
1 teaspoon soda
1/2 teaspoon salt
1/2 cup sugar
1/2 cup firmly packed brown
  sugar
48 milk chocolate candy
  kisses

1/2 cup shortening
1/2 cup peanut butter
1 egg
2 tablespoons milk
1 teaspoon vanilla

Combine all ingredients except candy in large mixer bowl. Mix on lowest speed until dough forms. Shape into balls, roll in sugar. Bake at 375° for 10 to 12 minutes. Remove from oven and top each cookie with a candy kiss.

Eleanor Allen Duncan
Austell, Georgia
Mrs. L. Stephen Mitchell (Linda)

247

CHOCOLATE PEANUT BUTTER CHIP COOKIES

Oven: 350° 8 to 9 minutes   Yield: 4 dozen cookies

1 1/4 cups margarine
1 3/4 cups sugar
2 eggs
2 teaspoons vanilla extract
2 cups all-purpose flour

3/4 cup cocoa
1 teaspoon baking soda
1/2 teaspoon salt
1 (12 oz.) package peanut
  butter baking chips

Cream butter and sugar until well blended. Add eggs and vanilla mixing well. Combine flour, cocoa, baking soda and salt. Gradually blend dry mixture into butter mixture. Stir in peanut butter chips. Drop by teaspoonfuls onto ungreased cookie sheet. Bake 8 to 9 minutes. Remove from cookie sheet and cool completely. Cookies will be chewy and moist.

Mrs. L. Stephen Mitchell (Linda)

COWBOY COOKIES

Oven: 350° 9 minutes   Yield: 4 to 5 dozen

1 cup butter or margarine
1 cup brown sugar
1 cup sugar
2 eggs
1 teaspoon vanilla
2 cups plain flour
1 teaspoon baking soda

1 teaspoon baking powder
1 teaspoon salt
1 teaspoon cinnamon
2 cups oatmeal
1 cup chopped nuts
1 cup raisins
2 cups chocolate chips

Cream butter, brown sugar, sugar, eggs and vanilla until light and fluffy. Add the remaining ingredients and stir until blended well. Drop a well-rounded teaspoon of dough onto a greased cookie sheet. Bake 350° for 9 minutes.

Mrs. Walter M. Lonergan II (Ginny)

DADDY'S OATMEAL COOKIES

Oven: 350° 10 minutes   Yield: 2 dozen cookies

1 cup plain flour	1/2 cup brown sugar
1/2 teaspoon salt	1 egg
1/2 teaspoon soda	2 teaspoons honey
1 teaspoon cinnamon	1 cup pecans
1/2 cup Crisco	1 cup raisins
1/2 cup sugar	1 1/2 cups oatmeal

Preheat oven to 350°. Mix together flour, salt, soda and cinnamon. Cream shortening. Add sugar, brown sugar and egg. Slowly add flour mixture; then honey, nuts, raisins and oatmeal.

Bake on lightly greased cookie sheet for 10 minutes.

Mrs. Hugh Farmer, Jr. (Charlsie)

RANGER COOKIES

Oven: 350°   Yield: 80 to 90 cookies

2 sticks butter or margarine	1/2 teaspoon salt
1 cup brown sugar	1 tablespoon vanilla
1 cup white sugar	2 cups quick cooking oatmeal
2 eggs	2 cups crisp whole rice cereal
2 cups plain flour, sifted	1 cup coconut
1/2 teaspoon baking powder	1 cup chopped pecans
1 teaspoon baking soda	pecan halves

Cream butter with sugar, add eggs and mix well. Sift flour with salt, baking powder and soda; add to creamed mixture. Stir in vanilla and mix well. Add oatmeal, rice cereal and chopped nuts. (This makes a stiff dough.) With teaspoon cut off small portion of dough and roll into balls using a little flour on hands. Place about 2 inches apart on cookie sheet, slightly oiled. Press each cookie down with half pecan and bake at 350° until brown. Cool thoroughly before storing.

Mrs. J.W. Owens (Elon)

GINGERBREAD BOYS

Oven: 375° 5 to 6 minutes   Yield: 60 servings

1 cup shortening (do not use margarine)	1 1/2 teaspoons soda
1 cup sugar	1/2 teaspoon salt
1 egg	2 to 3 teaspoons cinnamon
1 cup molasses	1 teaspoon ginger
2 tablespoons vinegar	1 teaspoon cloves
5 cups flour	Red cinnamon candies or raisins

Cream shortening and sugar well. Stir in egg, molasses, and vinegar; beat well. Stir together dry ingredients; stir into molasses mixture. Chill at least 3 hours. On lightly floured surface, roll dough to 1/8-inch thickness. Cut with gingerbread boy cutter. Place 1 inch apart on greased cookie sheet. Use cinnamon candies for faces and buttons. Bake 5 to 6 minutes in 375° oven. Cool slightly; remove from cookie sheet and cool on rack. Yields 60 4" cookies. May be decorated with white decorator's frosting. To hang on tree, cut tiny hole in top of cookie before baking. Put yarn or string through hole and hang on tree.

Mrs. Don Tomlinson (Jane)
Asheville, NC

JAN HAGEL KOEKJES
A traditional Dutch Cookie

Oven: 325 to 350° 25 minutes   Yield: 35 cookies

1 cup butter or butter flavored Crisco	Pinch of soda
1 cup sugar	1/2 teaspoon cinnamon
1 egg, separated	1/4 teaspoon salt
2 cups flour	Pecans or almonds, chopped

Cream butter and sugar, add unbeaten egg yolk. Add next four ingredients and spread in 10x15" cookie sheet. Beat egg white slightly and brush over the top. Sprinkle with more cinnamon and the nuts. Bake at 325 to 350° for 25 minutes. Cut while warm in any desired shape.

Mrs. David Kinrade (Joan)

PUMPKIN COOKIES

Oven: 350° 15 minutes   Yield: 5 to 6 dozen

1/2 cup margarine	1 teaspoon baking powder
1 1/2 cups sugar	1 teaspoon baking soda
1 egg	1/2 teaspoon salt
1 cup pumpkin (canned or cooked)	1 teaspoon nutmeg
	1 teaspoon cinnamon
1 teaspoon vanilla	1 cup (6 oz.) chocolate chips
2 1/2 cups all purpose flour	1/2 cup chopped nuts

Cream butter and sugar until light and fluffy. Beat in egg, pumpkin, and vanilla. Mix and sift flour, baking powder, baking soda, salt, nutmeg, and cinnamon. Add to creamed mixture. Mix well, then add nuts and chocolate chips. Mix well. Drop, by teaspoons, onto well-greased cookie sheet. Bake at 350° for 15 minutes or until light brown.

Betty Deason
Athens, Georgia

SUGAR COOKIES

Oven: 375° 12 minutes   Yield: 8 dozen cookies

1 cup butter	2 eggs
1 cup oil	4 cups all-purpose flour
1 cup sugar	1 teaspoon baking soda
1 cup powdered sugar	1 teaspoon cream of tartar
1 teaspoon vanilla	1 teaspoon salt

Combine butter, oil, sugars and vanilla in a large bowl. Beat until thoroughly creamed. Add eggs and beat well. Sift flour, baking soda, tartar and salt together. Add to creamed mixture and mix well. Chill at least 2 hours. Shape dough into small (1/2 teaspoon) balls and roll in sugar and place on lightly greased baking sheets. Bake at 375° for 12 minutes. Makes approximately 8 dozen.

Dough will keep in a sealed container in refrigerator for 2 weeks. Cookies can be frozen.

Mrs. Walter Lonergan, II (Ginny)

IN CLOVER LACE COOKIES

Yield: 2 dozen cookies

2 sticks butter (not
   margarine)
1 pound light brown sugar
2 1/4 cups quick-cooking
   oatmeal

3 tablespoons flour
1 teaspoon salt
1 egg, slightly beaten
1 teaspoon vanilla

Melt butter in 2-quart saucepan. Add brown sugar, stirring well with a large spoon. Add the remaining ingredients and stir well. Drop by level teaspoonfuls on well-buttered nonstick cookie sheets. Bake at 375° for about 5 minutes. Watch cookies closely; they should be golden brown. Let cookies cool for 30 seconds and remove with spatula onto racks to cool completely. If cookies mash together when removed, they are too warm. If they stick to the pan and break, they are too cool and need to be reheated briefly before removing them from the pan.

In Clover
LaGrange, Georgia

 ## ELM STREET SCHOOL BUTTER COOKIES

Oven: 350° for 10 to 12 minutes   Yield: 6-8 dozen cookies

1 pound butter
   (no margarine)
5 cups flour

1 cup powdered sugar
Dash salt
1 tablespoon vanilla

Cream butter. Add remaining ingredients, mixing well. Roll dough into log, wrap in aluminum foil, and refrigerate overnight. Slice into cookies and bake at 350° until very lightly browned, approximately 10 to 12 minutes.

Mrs. Eugene Jackson (Ruth)
Elm Street School

TEA CAKES

Oven: 325° 10 minutes   Yield: 7 dozen

1 cup shortening   1 teaspoon vanilla
1 cup sugar   2 1/2 cups self-rising flour
1 egg

Cream shortening and sugar. Add egg and vanilla, beating until just barely mixed. Add flour and mix dough well. Divide dough into 3 portions and roll into balls. Wrap balls in waxed paper and chill for 1 hour. (Dough may be kept in refrigerator up to 5 days). Take dough out of refrigerator and allow to stand for 10 minutes. Roll dough thin on floured board. Cut with seasonal cutters or use regular biscuit cutter. Cook for 10 minutes or until lightly browned in preheated oven. Store in air-tight container.

Mrs. Carlton Ingram (Grace)

CARAMEL BROWNIES

Oven: 350° 20 minutes   Yield: 2 dozen

1 cup flour   1 package Kraft caramels
1 cup oatmeal   5 tablespoons milk
3/4 cup butter   1/2 cup nuts
1/2 teaspoon baking soda   1 (6 ounce) package chocolate
1/4 teaspoon salt   chips

Blend first 5 ingredients together. Saving 3/4 cup of the mixture, spread remaining in a 9x13 pan. Bake 10 minutes at 350° and cool. Melt caramels and milk over low heat and spread over cooled crust. Sprinkle nuts and chocolate chips over caramel mixture. Top with 3/4 cup flour mixture. Bake additional 10 minutes at 350°.

Jennie L. Sellen

EASY FUDGE

Yield: 2 pounds

3 tablespoons butter
2/3 cup evaporated milk
1 1/2 cups sugar
1/3 cup corn syrup

1 8 ounce package semi-sweet
  chocolate
2 cups miniature
  marshmallows
1 teaspoon vanilla

In a 2 quart saucepan combine butter, evaporated milk, sugar, and corn syrup. Stirring constantly, cook over medium heat until mixture comes to a rolling boil. Stirring constantly, cook for 5 minutes. Remove from heat, add chocolate squares, marshmallows and vanilla to sauce pan. Stir vigorously until chocolate and marshmallows are melted. Pour into a buttered 8x8x2 inch pan. Chill in refrigerator about 1 hour or until firm. Cut into squares.

Be creative add—coconut
            nuts
            raisins
Whatever you like!

Mrs. Bill Wetmore (Vicki)

UNBELIEVABLE FUDGE
Creamy!

Yield: 2 dozen

2 boxes powdered sugar
1/2 cup cocoa
1 1/4 sticks butter

8 oz. Velveeta cheese
2 cups nuts
1 teaspoon vanilla

Sift sugar and cocoa together. Then melt butter and cheese over low heat or in microwave. Pour over sugar mixture. Add vanilla and nuts. Press into 8 or 9 inch pan. Chill.

Mrs. Douglas R. Hurley (Mildred)
Mrs. Duke Blackburn, Jr. (Lynn)

PEANUT BUTTER FUDGE
Won 1st prize at 1988 Coweta County Fair

Yield: 2 dozen

1 cup brown sugar, packed
1 cup granulated sugar
2/3 cup milk

1 teaspoon vanilla
2 heaping tablespoons creamy
    peanut butter

Place both cups sugar and milk into a saucepan. Bring to a boil, stirring constantly for exactly 3 minutes. Remove from heat. Add vanilla flavoring and peanut butter. Beat with electric mixer for 5 minutes. It is ready when the candy begins to stick to sides of pan. Pour onto a buttered platter and let harden at room temperature.

Important: Will not harden if crunchy peanut butter is used.

GRANDMA'S PEANUT BUTTER CANDY
Pinwheels that melt in your mouth

Yield: 24 individual pieces

3 tablespoons mashed
    potatoes, hot
1 box 10X powdered sugar

1/2 teaspoon salt
1 teaspoon vanilla
peanut butter, smooth

Slowly beat 3/4 box powdered sugar into the hot potatoes. Add salt and vanilla. When mixture is stiff like dough, roll out on remaining powdered sugar until about 1/4 inch thick. Dough should be oval shaped. Spread with smooth peanut butter. Roll up like a jelly roll from the long edge to resemble a large cigar. Slice and keep in airtight container to preserve freshness. (May use instant potatoes with boiling water for convenience, mixing to creamed potatoes consistency.)

Luine B. Miller

255

ENGLISH TOFFEE

Yield: 2 dozen

1 cup chopped pecans
2 sticks butter (not
  margarine)

1 cup sugar
1 (6 ounce) package
  semi-sweet chocolate chips

Grease cookie sheet. Sprinkle 1/3 cup chopped nuts on cookie sheet.

Using candy thermometer, cook butter and sugar to 300° (hard-crack stage), then spread on cookie sheet over nuts. Sprinkle chocolate over hot mixture and when it begins to melt, spread over candy. Sprinkle remaining nuts over chocolate.

Cool in refrigerator for about 1 hour. Crack candy into bite-size pieces and store in air-tight tin.

Mrs. Stephen L. Mitchell (Linda)

NEVER FAIL DIVINITY
Avoid making in rainy weather

Yield: 2 to 3 dozen

4 cups sugar
1 cup light corn syrup
3/4 cup water

3 egg whites, stiffly beaten
1 teaspoon vanilla
1 cup chopped pecans

Place sugar, corn syrup and water in saucepan over medium heat. Stir until sugar is dissolved. Cook without stirring until candy thermometer registers 255 degrees. Remove from heat and pour in a fine stream into the stiffly beaten egg whites, beating constantly. Continue beating until mixture holds its shape and loses its gloss. Add vanilla and pecans. Drop by teaspoonfuls onto waxed paper.

Jane C. Johnson
Fayetteville, GA

MICROWAVE CANDY

Yield: 24 1 1/2 inch cups

1 cup semi-sweet chocolate
   chips
1 cup peanut butter chips

2 tablespoons oil
1 cup unsalted cocktail
   peanuts

    Mix all ingredients except peanuts in glass mixing bowl. Microwave on high for 1 minute. Stir. Microwave on high for 30 seconds. Add 1 cup peanuts. Put in petit-four cups. Refrigerate until ready to serve.

Kay Kitchens Newman
Montgomery, Alabama

MICROWAVE CHOCOLATE SAUCE

Microwave: High

4 ounces chocolate chips
1/4 cup cocoa
1/2 cup water

Optional: 1/4 cup sherry,
   Grand Marnier, Amaretto,
   or Kahlua

    Combine ingredients and heat in microwave on high until hot and chips melt. Stir every 30 seconds. Stir in sherry or liqueur if desired.

Mrs. William M. Berry, III (Anne Jarrell)

HOMEMADE CHOCOLATE SAUCE

5 squares unsweetened
   chocolate
1 box confectioners sugar

1 can evaporated milk
1 stick margarine

    Place all ingredients in double boiler and cook over medium heat using whisk until smooth. Can be served hot over ice cream. Store in refrigerator. Reheat when needed.

Mrs. Chip Goen (Sallie)

EASY APPLE PIE
It can be made 12 hours ahead of time; slices won't be runny

Oven: 350° 25 minutes   Yield: 6 servings

5 apples
1 tablespoon lemon juice
3/4 cup sugar
2 tablespoons all-purpose
  flour
1 teaspoon ground cinnamon

Dash ground nutmeg
Dash of salt
2 (9-inch) Petz Pie Pastry
  Crust
2 tablespoons margarine
Milk

Peel, core and thinly slice apples. Sprinkle with lemon juice. Combine sugar, flour and spices. Mix with apples. Pour into pie shells and dot with margarine. Seal with second pie crust. Brush top of pie crust with milk and sprinkle a little sugar on top. Bake at 350° for 25 minutes. Let the pie cool before serving.

Mrs. Peter Gosch (Lisa)

PEACH ICE BOX PIE

Yield: 1 deep dish or 2 regular size pies

2 lemons (juice) or 1/4 cup
  concentrated lemon juice
1 can condensed milk
8 large peaches,
  approximately (chopped)

1 deep dish or 2 regular size
  pie shells
1/2 pint whipped cream or 1
  carton cool whip

Mix lemon juice and condensed milk. Add peaches. Pour into baked, cooled pie shell. Top with whipped topping.

Peaches should be very ripe. The amount of peaches can vary without affecting it. Should use only fresh peaches.

Mrs. Harvey Roberts (Carolyn)

PEANUT DREAM PIE

Yield: 1 pie

1 (8 ounce) package cream
  cheese
1 cup 4X sugar
1/2 cup crunchy peanut butter
1/2 cup milk
1 (9 ounce) carton frozen
  whipped topping (thawed)

1/4 cup chopped roasted
  peanuts
1/4 cup chocolate mini-chips
1 (9-inch) graham cracker
  crust or baked pie crust

Mix cream cheese until soft and fluffy. Mix in peanut butter and sugar. Add milk slowly until well blended. Fold topping into mixture. Add peanuts and chocolate chips, saving a few for sprinkling on top. Ladle into pie crust and freeze firm.

Mrs. Don Tomlinson (Jane)

MOCK KEY LIME PIE

Yield: 4 to 6 servings

1 small package Jello gelatin
  (lime)
1 cup hot water
1/4 cup sugar
1/4 cup lime juice

1/4 cup water
1 pint vanilla ice cream,
  softened
1 graham cracker crust,
  already prepared

Dissolve Jello in cup of hot water, add sugar and lime juice and water (1/4 cup) with big spoon, cut ice cream into mixture, pour into graham cracker crust and refrigerate.

Mrs. Larry Deason (Sharon)

PUMPKIN CHEESE PIE

Oven: 375° 30 minutes
            15 minutes   Yield: 6 to 8 servings

1 (8 ounce) cream cheese,
   softened
3/4 cup packed brown sugar
2 tablespoons flour
1 teaspoon cinnamon
1 teaspoon ginger
1/2 teaspoon salt

1/4 teaspoon nutmeg
1 (16 ounce) canned pumpkin
1 (5.33 ounce) can
   evaporated milk
3 eggs
1 (9 inch) unbaked pie crust

Topping:

2 tablespoons butter
1/3 cup brown sugar

3/4 cup walnuts, chopped

Preheat oven to 350°. In large bowl with mixer at medium, beat cream cheese and next 6 ingredients. Add pumpkin, undiluted milk, and eggs. Beat just until blended. Pour into pie crust. Bake 30 minutes. Prepare topping by melting butter and stirring in nuts and brown sugar. Spoon topping over pie. Bake 15 minutes longer. Cool pie. Refrigerate leftovers.

Mrs. Larry Deason (Sharon)

What moistens the lip,
And what brightens the eye,
What calls back the past
Like rich pumpkin pie?

John Greenleaf Whittier

Pusher
Helps little hands get food onto a fork or spoon.

CHILDREN

BARBECUE CUPS

Oven: 400° 10 to 12 minutes   Yield: 6 servings

1 pound ground beef
1 tablespoon minced onion
1/2 cup barbecue sauce
1 1/2 tablespoons brown
  sugar

1 (8 ounce) can biscuits
3/4 cup shredded cheese

Sauté beef and onions; stir in barbecue sauce and sugar. Place biscuit in greased muffin pan, pressing to cover bottom and sides. Spoon meat mixture into cups and sprinkle with cheese. Bake in 400° oven for 10 to 12 minutes.

Julie Bedford

GIRL SCOUT SPECIAL

Oven: 400° 60 minutes   Yield: 4 servings

1 pound ground beef, lean
8 medium potatoes, diced
1 onion sliced
Salt to taste

Pepper to taste
Garlic to taste
2-3 carrots, sliced (optional)

Make four patties from the ground beef. Place each one on a separate piece of aluminum foil. Place a slice of onion on top with potatoes around the patty. (Add carrots with potatoes.) Add salt, pepper and garlic. Fold and close each and place on a baking dish. Cook at 400° for one hour. (Note: may need more spices for adults.)

Mrs. Hal Williams (Penny)

CHICKEN ROLL-UPS

Oven: 350° 30 minutes   Yield: 6 to 8 servings

1 8-oz. package crescent
dinner rolls
2 cups chopped, cooked
chicken or turkey
1 cup (4 ozs.) shredded sharp
cheddar cheese

1 can (10 3/4 oz.) cream of
celery soup, undiluted
1 can milk (measure in soup
can)
1 2-oz. jar pimiento, chopped
and drained (optional)

Separate rolls; combine chopped chicken and cheese. (*Reserve about half of this mixture for use in the sauce). Place about 3 tablespoons of the remaining chicken, cheese mixture on each individual roll, then roll up. Place roll-ups seam side down (points down) in a lightly greased 7 1/2x11 3/4" baking dish. Mix soup and milk together. Add reserved chicken cheese mixture. Add pimientos, if desired. Pour over roll-ups and bake at 350° for 30 minutes.

Mrs. Mike Barber (Julia)

CRESCENT CHILI ROLL UPS

Oven: 425°

1 pound ground beef
1 cup grated cheese
1 egg (beaten)

1 1/2 teaspoons salt
Chili powder to taste
2 cans crescent rolls

Brown ground beef and drain. Mix cheese, egg, salt and chili powder with beef. Pull crescent rolls apart. Put spoonful of mixture into rolls and fold over and seal. Grease a cookie sheet and bake in a 425° oven until brown.

Betty Ayers

CHILI-CHEESEBURGER PIE

Oven: 400° 30 minutes   Serves: 4 to 6 servings

1 pound ground beef
1 1/2 cups chopped onion
1/2 teaspoon salt
1 1/2 teaspoons chili powder

1 cup shredded sharp cheddar
  cheese
1 cup milk
1/2 cup Bisquick Mix
2 eggs

Lightly grease one 9″ pie plate. Brown ground beef and onion, then pour off any excess grease. Stir in salt and chili powder. Spread in pie plate. Sprinkle with cheese. Beat remaining ingredients until smooth, either 15 seconds on high speed in blender or 1 minute by hand. Pour into pie plate. Bake at 400° about 30 minutes. Let stand 5 minutes before cutting.

Mrs. Mike Spitler (Rita)

SPOON BURGERS

Yield: 6 servings

1 onion, chopped
2 tablespoons vinegar
2 tablespoons butter
2 tablespoons brown sugar
1 tablespoon lemon juice
2 pounds ground beef

1 cup water
1 cup tomato catsup
2 teaspoons salt
3 tablespoons worcestershire
  sauce

Fry together the onion, vinegar, butter, brown sugar, lemon juice and ground beef until the beef is brown. Add the remaining ingredients. Cover and simmer 45 minutes. Spoon into hamburger buns.

GROUND BEEF & POTATO CASSEROLE

Oven: 350° 25 to 30 minutes   Yield: 6 servings

1 medium onion
1 1/2 lbs. ground beef
5 medium potatoes
2 cans cream of mushroom
 soup

2/3 cup milk
1 teaspoon garlic powder
Salt & pepper to taste
8 oz. cheddar cheese

Cut up onion and brown with ground beef. Slice potatoes into round sections and boil until done. Grease casserole dish. Mix soup, milk, garlic powder, salt and pepper. Put 1/2 of potatoes in dish, add 1/2 of drained ground beef and put 1/2 mixture of soup and milk on top. Grate quantity of cheese desired and sprinkle on top. Start over with layer of potatoes, ground beef, soup/milk and top with cheese. Bake at 350° for 25 to 30 minutes.

Mrs. Dennis McEntire (Sally)

PIZZA WHEELS

Yield: 12 servings

1 1/2 lbs. hot sausage
1 lb. Velveeta Cheese
1 tablespoon catsup
1 dash worcestershire sauce

Dash oregano
Dash garlic salt
6 English muffins

Brown sausage. Add remaining ingredients until cheese melts. Let cool and spread on English muffin halves. May be frozen individually to use for children's lunch. Must be microwaved at lunch time. Put frozen pizza wheel in lunch box, by noon just microwave till hot, 30 to 45 sec.

Mrs. Scott Markham (Carol)

BAKED BEANS

Oven: 450° 30 to 40 minutes

1 garlic minced (or onion)	1 teaspoon mustard
1 teaspoon oil	1 large can pork & beans
1/2 lb. ground beef	Dash salt & pepper
1/4 cup catsup	2 slices of bacon
2 tablespoons brown sugar	

Brown meat in oil, add garlic (or onion), simmer slightly, take from heat and mix with other ingredients. Pour in baking dish or bean pot placing bacon on top and cook in 450° oven about 30 or 40 minutes.

Mrs. Max Garrison

MICROWAVE MACARONI AND CHEESE

Microwave: 1 to 1.3 minutes
3 minutes
4 to 6 minutes   Yield: 4 servings

1 (8 ounce) box of elbow macaroni	1 teaspoon dry mustard
2 tablespoons butter	1/2 teaspoon salt and pepper
2 tablespoons all-purpose flour	Dash garlic powder
1 tablespoon minced onion	1 1/2 cups milk
	2 cups shredded cheese

Cook macaroni and drain. Place butter in a 3 quart glass dish. Cook 1 to 1.3 minutes in microwave. Stir in flour, onion, mustard, salt, pepper and garlic. Gradually stir in milk. Microwave 3 minutes, stirring every minute. Stir in cheese, then macaroni. Cover and microwave 4 to 6 minutes. Let stand 3 minutes before serving.

Mrs. Larry Deason (Sharon)

JELLO BLOCKS

Yield: 100 small squares

3 (3 ounce) packages gelatin (any flavor, regular or sugar free)

4 envelopes unflavored gelatin
4 cups boiling water

Combine gelatins in a large bowl. Add boiling water and stir until completely dissolved. Pour into a 13x9″ pan and chill until firm. Cut into squares. Can be picked up and eaten with fingers.

For jello shapes pour into 2 13x9″ pans and chill then cut out with cookie cutters.

For party or special treat, cut jello out with gingerbread man cookie cutter and let children decorate with whipped cream and decorative candies.

Mrs. Don Tomlinson (Jane)
Asheville, North Carolina

BABY JUICE GELLIES

Yield: 10 to 20 gellies

1 envelope unflavored gelatin

2 small bottles baby juice, any flavor

In a small saucepan, sprinkle gelatin over juice. Let stand 1 minute. Stir over low heat until gelatin is completely dissolved, about 3 minutes. Pour into small pan and chill until firm. Cut into squares or fancy shapes for finger eating.

Miss Katie Barber
Miss Laura Barber

Rainy day activity: Paint animal cookies with evaporated milk to which food coloring has been added.

FRUIT KABOBS

Grapes*	Strawberries
Blueberries*	Pineapple chunks
Banana chunks	Miniature marshmallows
Kiwi chunks	

Place fruit on skewer. Place on cookie sheet and freeze until solid. Cover with plastic wrap. When serving, finish off with marshmallows.

Variation: Use king-size, colored party toothpicks for snack version.

*Not for small children

Miss Wade Nichols
Miss Ann Forrest Nichols

ENERGY CANDY
Great snack for children

Yield: 12 dozen

1 cup honey	2 cups raisins, optional
1 cup peanut butter	1 cup chopped nuts, optional
2 cups non-fat dry milk	

Mix honey and peanut butter in bowl. Gradually add dry milk, mixing well. Mix in raisins and nuts. Shape into log; wrap. Chill until firm. To serve, cut into 1/2 inch slices. Keep refrigerated.

If preferred, candy may be rolled into 1 inch balls and rolled in coconut or oatmeal.

Mrs. Don Tomlinson (Jane)
Asheville, North Carolina

COTTAGE CHEESE PANCAKES
Quick nourishing breakfast for kids

Yield: 6 to 8 servings

1 pint cottage cheese (regular
  or light)
6 eggs

1/3 cup flour
1/2 teaspoon salt

Beat eggs. Add cottage cheese, flour and salt and mix well. On hot oiled griddle, spoon mixture by tablespoonfuls to make small pancakes (about 3 inches in diameter). Turn when pancakes begin to get dry around the edges. They should be very lightly browned. Serve with butter or syrup.

Mrs. Sam O. Candler
Sharpsburg, Georgia

FROZEN FLOWER POTS
Makes a hit at end of year school picnic or birthday party

Yield: 10 servings

1 large package Oreo cookies
1/4 cup butter, melted
1/2 gallon vanilla or
  chocolate ice cream,
  softened

10 (3 inch) clay pots
10 "gummie" worms
10 flowers (plastic or made
  from construction paper &
  green pipe cleaners)

Crush Oreos in food processor. Add melted butter. Fill bottom fourth of each pot with Oreo mixture. Add softened ice cream, leaving top fourth of pot for Oreo mixture. Top off with Oreos. Before serving, decorate with worms and flowers. Pots can be personalized or decorated beforehand with paint markers.

Miss Marion Ellis Berry

NUTTY PEANUT BUTTER ICE CREAM BAR

Yield: 6 bars

1 pint vanilla ice cream,
  softened
1/4 cup peanut butter, creamy
3/4 cup roasted peanuts,
  chopped

3/4 cup chocolate topping
6 (5 ounce) paper cups
6 popsicle sticks

In a mixing bowl blend ice cream and peanut butter together. Place one tablespoon peanuts in bottom of paper cup. Spread one tablespoon chocolate over peanuts and spoon in 1/4 cup ice cream. Repeat procedure, ending with ice cream. Insert popsicle stick and freeze. To serve, remove paper cup.

Frank Jarrell Berry
Maybeth Graham Marchman

EASY CHOCOLATE BLOCKS

Yield: 6 dozen pieces

4 envelopes gelatin
1/2 cup sugar
1 1/2 cups cold water

1 package (12 ounces)
    semi-sweet chocolate pieces

Combine all ingredients in a medium saucepan. Stir constantly over low heat 5 minutes, or until chocolate is melted. Pour into 8 or 9 inch square pan and chill until firm. To serve cut into 1 inch squares.

Mrs. Larry Deason (Sharon)

LEMONADE PIE

Yield: 8 servings

1 small can frozen lemonade
1 (9 ounce) Cool Whip

1 can Eagle Brand condensed
    milk
1 graham cracker pie shell

Set lemonade aside to partially thaw. Combine all ingredients, mixing well. Pour into pie shell and refrigerate until ready to serve.

Betty Ayers

Then Mrs. Tiggy-Winkle made tea—a cup for herself and a cup for Lucie. They sat before the fire on a bench and looked sideways at one another.

Beatrix Potter

PEANUT BUTTER PLAY DOUGH

1 cup peanut butter   1 cup powdered milk
1 cup honey   1 cup oatmeal

Combine ingredients in a large bowl. Mix with spoon then knead with hands. If mixture is too sticky, add more milk and oatmeal in equal amounts until mixture is consistency for modeling. Harden your creation in refrigerator. Then eat it for dessert!

Mrs. Robert L. Montgomery, Jr. (Cindy)

CRACKER JACKS

Oven: 250° 1 hour

2 cups (1 box) brown sugar   1 cup butter or margarine
1/2 cup Karo syrup   1/2 teaspoon baking soda
1/2 teaspoon salt   4 to 6 quarts popcorn, popped
1 teaspoon vanilla extract   2 cups peanuts

Combine brown sugar, Karo syrup, salt, vanilla extract, and butter in sauce pan and bring to boil. Cook 5 minutes, then add baking soda. Watch mixture carefully because it will foam. Mix popcorn and peanuts together. Pour mixture over popcorn and spread on a cookie sheet. Bake at 250° for one hour, stirring 3 or 4 times.

Mrs. Walter Lonergan, II (Ginny)

Roll balls of vanilla ice cream in grated coconut or chopped nuts. Store in freezer and serve with chocolate sauce and whipped cream.

MOM'S ICE BOX COOKIES

Oven: 400° 10 to 12 minutes   Yield: 2 dozen cookies

3 eggs	Pinch of salt
1 pound butter	1 teaspoon baking powder
1 cup sugar	6 cups flour
1 cup brown sugar	1 cup nuts
1 teaspoon soda (dissolved in	1 cup colored cherries
1 teaspoon hot water)	1 teaspoon cinnamon

Mix all ingredients together. Make into 4 rolls, wrap in wax paper, place in freezer for 24 hours. When ready to bake roll in colored sugar. Slice and bake at 400° for 10 to 12 minutes.

Mrs. William Wallace (Ruth)

CHRISTMAS COOKIES (CUT-OUTS)

Oven: 350° 10 to 12 minutes   Yield: 6 dozen

1 cup butter or margarine	1 teaspoon soda
1 1/2 cups sugar	1 teaspoon cream of tartar
2 eggs	1 teaspoon vanilla
3 cups flour	

Beat butter, sugar and eggs until fluffy. Add flour, soda, cream of tartar and vanilla and mix well. Chill well (overnight if possible). Roll very thin on floured board. Cut with floured cookie cutters and bake on greased cookie tins in 350° oven for 10 to 12 minutes. Cool before decorating.

Mrs. Scott Markham (Carol)

Dress up plain oatmeal with colored sugar or cinnamon.

REINDEER SANDWICH
Pretty as well as nutritious

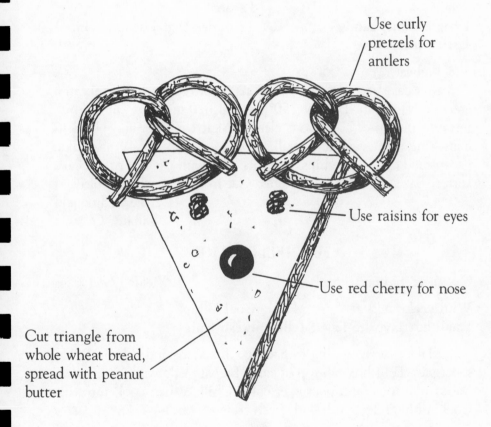

Use curly pretzels for antlers

Use raisins for eyes

Use red cherry for nose

Cut triangle from whole wheat bread, spread with peanut butter

TURTLE CAKE

Oven: 350° 15 to 20 minutes
    350° 20 minutes   Yield: 20 squares

1 box German chocolate cake   **1 small can evaporated milk**
  mix   **Pecans**
1 bag caramel candy   **12 ounce bag chocolate chips**
1 stick margarine

Preheat oven to 350°.

Mix cake according to directions on box. Pour 1/2 of mix in a greased 9x13″ pan. Bake at 350° for 15 to 20 minutes, (until knife inserted in center comes out clean). Melt caramels and blend in margarine and evaporated milk. Pour over baked cake. Sprinkle pecans and chocolate chips over this. Top with the rest of the cake batter. Bake again for 20 minutes. Cut in squares when cooled.

Debbie Bedingfield
Dublin, Georgia

FUN JELLO CAKE

Oven: According to package   Yield: 12 servings

White cake mix   **Cool Whip**
Small box favorite flavor Jello   **Fresh fruit**

Make cake according to package directions and bake in 9x13″ sheet pan. Poke holes in top of cake. Prepare Jello with 1/4 cup less water than usual and pour over cake. Chill. When cool, top with Cool Whip and garnish with fresh fruit.

Roy Owen Jackson

Children love to string fruit loops or cheerios on yarn; then wear and eat.

SCHOOL DAZE PUNCH

Yield: 25 servings

1 package (2 quart)
pre-sweetened fruit flavored
drink mix (such as
Kool-Aid)
1 quart water

46 ounce can fruit juice (may
use pineapple, orange,
grapefruit or combination)
1 quart Sprite or ginger ale

Mix above ingredients. Chill and serve with ice. May be mixed several hours before serving time. When picking drink mix flavor, consider the color your fruit drink mix will turn when combined with the juice.

Emily Parrott

A FROSTED ORANGE
A nutritious drink for children

Yield: 4 (10 ounce) servings

1 (6 ounce) can frozen fruit
  juice
1/2 cup sugar
1 cup water

1 cup milk
1/4 to 1/2 teaspoon vanilla
  extract, optional

Put all ingredients into blender. Fill rest of blender with ice cubes. Blend until ice is crushed and drink is frothy.

Miss Ellen Barber
Miss Beth Barber

SILLY PUTTY
Not to be eaten

White school glue (Elmer's)   **Food coloring (optional)**
Liquid starch (Sta Flo)

Mix and knead equal parts of glue and starch. Add food coloring, if desired. Store in airtight container.

Mrs. Robert Montgomery (Cindy)

PLAYDOUGH
Not to be eaten

1 cup flour   **Few drops of food coloring**
2 teaspoons cream of tartar   **1/2 cup salt**
1 cup water   **1 tablespoon oil**

Mix in saucepan. Cook on medium heat, stirring until thickened (takes only a few minutes and looks quite gooey). While still warm, knead a little. Keep in a covered container when not in use to keep from hardening.

Maybe it's always pepper that makes people hot tempered . . . and vinegar that makes them sour—and camomile that makes them bitter—and—and—barley sugar and such things that make children sweet-tempered. I only wish people knew **that**.

Lewis Carroll

SOAP CRAYONS

Yield: each cup of Ivory Snow
makes 2 crayons

Ivory Snow   **Food coloring**

Put 1/8 cup of water in a 2 cup Pyrex measuring cup. Add 1/2 bottle of food coloring (1 1/2 oz). Add Ivory Snow to make 1 cup. Stir until all the soap is moistened well. Take out and knead in hands until soap turns a solid color, no white left. Roll into two crayons shape logs and let harden for at least a day.

Group or Party Method: Ahead of time: Put 1 cup of Ivory Snow in a sturdy one gallon size plastic bag, (one for each child). When ready to make crayons add the (1/8 cup) colored water. Squeeze bag until mixture turns a solid color. Take out and roll into crayons.

Rinse hands right away and soap and color will wash off.

William M. Berry, IV

SOAP BUBBLES

2 cups warm water   **1 tablespoon glycerin (found**
2 tablespoons liquid detergent   **at drug store)**
1 tablespoon sugar

Combine and keep in covered container.

Mrs. Robert Montgomery (Cindy)

Child's Set - Feeding Spoon
                  Spoon
                  Fork
                  Pusher

MACARONI NECKLACES

Macaroni   Food coloring

Soak macaroni in colored water about 5 minutes, until it turns desired color. Drain. Lay on wax paper, separating macaroni so they will not stick together. When dry, string on yarn. Store in air tight container.

Mrs. Terry Lunsford (Frances)

REINDEER FOOD
Not to be eaten by humans

Oatmeal   Plastic sandwich bags
Red and green glitter   Red ribbon

In each bag put 1/3 cup oatmeal and sprinkle in glitter. Tie bag with red ribbon and attach the following directions:

On Christmas Eve, just before bedtime, take package of Reindeer food outside. Untie package. Make a wish as you are turning around in a circle, throwing reindeer food evenly onto lawn. Go inside to bed and wait for Santa Claus to come and see if your wish comes true.

Miss Rosemary Goen

EASTER EGG DYE

1/4 teaspoon food coloring   Hard boiled eggs
1 tablespoon vinegar   Crayons, markers, glue
3/4 cup boiling water   Glitter: optional

Add food coloring and vinegar to 3/4 cup boiling water. Add hard boiled egg and turn with a spoon until it colors. Remove egg with spoon and let dry. If decorating egg with crayons, do so before dying them. If using markers or glitter, wait until dyed eggs are dry.

Miss Maybeth Graham Marchman
Master Frank Jarrell Berry

CARNIVAL IDEAS

BEAN BAG TOSS

Use any type of wood board with painting on it such as a clown with balloons, tree with apples, etc. Have at least three holes cut for bean bags to be thrown through.

WATER GUN SQUIRT

Have a bucket full of water. Take styrofoam and cut out hole to fit votive candle. Let children try to squirt out the candles with squirt gun.

RING TOSS

Fill 2 liter coke bottles with sand. Using rings such as crochet hoops, try to toss the ring around the neck of the bottles.

APPLE BOB

All children love to bob for apples, but if it's too cold to get wet, then hang apples from ceiling or tree on a string and swing the string. Let them try to catch the apples in their mouths.

GO FISHING

A favorite for little children because everyone gets a prize. Take a large box such as a refrigerator box and paint fish scene on outside. Take 1/2 inch dowel rods, attach string and paper cup or clothes pin to end for putting prizes in or on.

PICK A PRIZE

This can be done on a tree or a person with an apron with lots of pockets. Wrap small prizes and hang on tree for children to pick off or have prizes in pockets for children to choose a pocket.

DUCK PICK

Another favorite with small children. Take floating rubber ducks and put numbers or letters on the bottoms. Float in a large bucket. The child picks up a duck. The prizes correspond to the numbers or letters on the bottom of the ducks.

PINATA

Buy or make your own pinata to allow children to break open and get prizes. To make your own pinata wrap balloon with papier mâché strips leaving a hole through which to fill pinata. When dry, pop balloon and fill with goodies. Tape over hole and paint.

It is very nice to think
The world is full of meat and drink,
With little children saying grace
In every Christian kind of place.

Robert Louis Stevenson

GRAHAM CRACKER HOUSE

ICING:

3 egg whites, beaten with 1/2 teaspoon cream of tartar. Add 1 box confectioner's sugar, 1/2 cup at a time. Beat 8 minutes. Keep icing covered with damp cloth. Will make enough for 6 houses, or 4 if children put on icing. Put spot of icing everywhere you want to stick decorations. Cover whole roof with icing.

GRAHAM CRACKERS:

Use half a cracker for all sides and propped together for roof.

Cut a half cracker diagonally for front and back roof.

Put the house together with icing and let it harden a while before decorating. It will probably set in an hour.

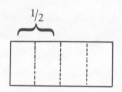

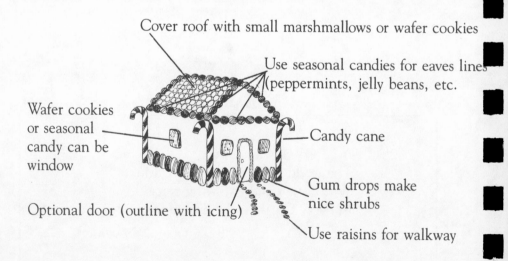

Cover roof with small marshmallows or wafer cookies

Use seasonal candies for eaves lines (peppermints, jelly beans, etc.

Wafer cookies or seasonal candy can be window

Candy cane

Gum drops make nice shrubs

Optional door (outline with icing)

Use raisins for walkway

EARTH DAY DIRT CAKE

This can be made in a large flower pot or individual pots. For a boy's birthday party, it is cute in a dump truck. Gummy worms can be added for effect.

Yield: 10 to 12 servings

1 large bag Oreo cookies
1/2 cup butter
1 cup powdered sugar
1 (8 ounce) package cream
   cheese
3 1/3 cups milk

2 (3 1/2 ounce) packages
French vanilla instant
pudding
1 (8 ounce) frozen whipped
topping

Crush Oreos in food processor. Cream together butter, sugar, and cream cheese. In separate bowl, mix together milk, pudding and whipped topping. Combine the two mixtures. Alternate layers of mixture and cookie crumbs in clean flowerpot, starting and ending with cookie crumbs. Chill or freeze.

Eleanor Haynes

MERRY-GO-ROUND CUPCAKES

Cupcakes
Small paper parasols (used for
   drink garnishes)

Animal crackers

Put one parasol in the center of each cupcake. Arrange animal crackers around edges. Be careful if you add a candle.

Miss Ann Forrest Nichols
Miss Wade Nichols

And instead of a nice dish of minnows they had a roasted grasshopper with lady-bird sauce, which frogs consider a beautiful treat; but I think it must have been nasty!

Beatrix Potter

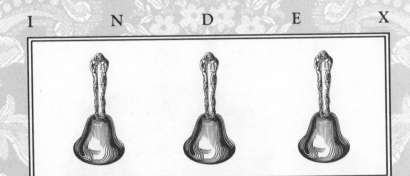

Dinner Bell

"That all softening, overpowering knell,
The tocsin of the soul—the dinner bell."

Bryan

288

INDEX

INDEX

INDEX

INDEX

NEWNAN JUNIOR SERVICE LEAGUE
ACTIVE MEMBERS
1993-1994

Mrs. David Asher (Tammy)
Mrs. Randy Beckom (Ginger)
Mrs. Hank Blanton (Brenda)
Mrs. Michael Booth (Laurie)
Mrs. Mark Brown (Toni)
Mrs. Brad Byrum (Elizabeth)
Mrs. David Clark (Anne)
Mrs. Jimmy Craft (Polly)
Mrs. Joe Crain, Jr. (Sandee)
Mrs. Paul Davis (Angela)
Mrs. Scott Douglas (Julianne)
Mrs. Craig Duncan (Romelle)
Mrs. Randall Duncan (Beth)
Mrs. Frank Eldridge (Edie)
Mrs. Craig Evans (Suanne)
Mrs. Frank Farmer (Melody)
Mrs. Allen Farrish (Rudy)
Mrs. David Frank (Carol)
Mrs. Tom Freeman (Michelle)
Mrs. Preston Fulmer, Jr. (Ivey)
Mrs. Mitch Ginn (Mary Jane)
Mrs. Richard Gunnels (Melinda)
Mrs. Britt Hall (Jennifer)
Mrs. Larry Harkleroad (Jennifer)
Mrs. Steve Harris (Frances)
Mrs. Peter Hayes (Natalie)
Mrs. Joe Helm (Beverly)
Mrs. Steve Hendrix (Chris)
Mrs. Wesley Howard (Mary)
Mrs. Alan Huckaby (Josie)
Mrs. Glen LaForce (Jill)
Mrs. David LaGuardia (Jane)
Mrs. Rick LaGuardia (Cathy)

Mrs. Gary Lawrence (Julie)
Mrs. Jim Lawson (Peggie)
Mrs. H. Russell Lester, III (Elizabeth)
Mrs. Joe Lowery (Cathy)
Mrs. Jim Luckie (Cindy)
Mrs. William McGuire (Ginny)
Mrs. Dan MacManus (Mollie)
Mrs. Mac McKinney (Julie)
Mrs. Steve McLain (Patty)
Mrs. Wayne Martin (Stacia)
Mrs. Rick Melville (Rita)
Mrs. Edmond Miller (Frances)
Mrs. John Myers (Robin)
Mrs. Lee Pettet (Kelly)
Mrs. Don Phillips (Ann)
Mrs. Stan Price (Kern)
Mrs. Steve Register (Susan)
Mrs. Wayne Robertson (Carol)
Mrs. Frank Robinson (Eva)
Mrs. Mitchell Sherwood (Cindy)
Mrs. Earl Smith (Melanie)
Mrs. Stephen Sprayberry (Colleen)
Mrs. Mark Staley (Connie)
Mrs. Kent Stier (Joy)
Mrs. Eric Stipe (Kathy)
Mrs. Frank Sullivan (Lynn)
Mrs. Jim Taylor (Sally)
Mrs. Lee Troutman (Nan)
Mrs. Keith Troxler (Beth)
Mrs. John Tucker (Carol)
Mrs. Richard Westerfield (Jay)
Mrs. Win Wise (Kim)
Mrs. Mark Wood (Becky)

NEWNAN JUNIOR SERVICE LEAGUE
SUSTAINERS
1993-1994

Mrs. Jimmy Adams (Brenda) (85)
Mrs. Joe Almon (Deena) (88)
Mrs. Cliff Arnett (Carol) (84)
Mrs. William Banks (Betty) (88)
Mrs. Michael Barber (Julia) (91)
Mrs. William Berry, III (Anne) (91)
Mrs. Duke Blackburn (Lynn) (93)
Mrs. Jerry Boren (Nelda) (87)
Mrs. Tony Brogdon (Wendy) (90)
Mrs. Charlie Brown (Pam) (87)
Mrs. Tim Carrol (Beth) (93)
Mrs. Thomas Carson (Nancy) (90)
Mrs. Ned Chambless (Jane) (87)
Mrs. Roddy Clifton (Connie) (92)
Mrs. Robert Cordle (Mitzi) (90)
Mrs. David Cotton (Pat) (93)
Mrs. Robert Cox (Louise) (86)
Mrs. John Herbert Cranford (Carolyn)(93)
Mrs. Larry Deason (Sharon) (90)
Mrs. Joseph Distel (Pat) (84)
Mrs. Steve Fanning (Diane)
Mrs. Herman Fletcher (Anne)
Mrs. Fred Gilbert (Ann)
Mrs. Jack Giles (Pam) (86)
Mrs. Richard Glover (Debbie) (86)
Mrs. Peter Gosch (Lisa) (92)
Mrs. Joe Harless (Carol) (86)
Mrs. Bill Hartselle (Joan) (92)
Mrs. Hugh Heflin, Jr. (Julia) (92)
Mrs. Larry Huggins (Missy) (88)
Mrs. Alan W. Jackson (Leigh) (91)
Mrs. E.H. Johnson, II (Marie) (86)
Mrs. Stanley Lanier (Debbie) (89)
Mrs. Walter Lonergan (Ginny) (92)
Mrs. Terry Lunsford (Frances) (91)
Mrs. Frank Marchman (Beth) (91)
Mrs. Scott Markham (Carol) (92)
Mrs. Dennis McEntire (Sally) (92)
Mrs. Robert Merrell (Sam) (93)

Mrs. Robin Miller (Alice) (86)
Mrs. Stephen Mitchell (Linda) (92)
Mrs. David Morgan (Linda) (86)
Mrs. Thomas Morningstar (Donna)
Mrs. Joseph Morris (Linda) (86)
Mrs. Harry Mullins (Susan) (87)
Mrs. Hutch Murphey (Mary Jane) (93)
Mrs. Andrew Muzio (Eileen) (91)
Mrs. James Palmer (Maude) (85)
Mrs. Jim Parks (Betty)
Mrs. David Parrott (Carol) (84)
Mrs. Joe Powell (Cathy) (92)
Mrs. Scott Reeves (Sammy) (89)
Mrs. Mayo Royal, Jr. (Nancy) (90)
Mrs. Bob Sandlin (Pam) (92)
Mrs. Rhodes Shell (Kathy) (85)
Mrs. Neal Shepard (Jodie) (84)
Mrs. Lee Simpson (Sey) (87)
Mrs. Charles V. Slomka (Tricia) (92)
Mrs. Donald Sprayberry, Jr. (Terri) (89)
Mrs. Bob Stitt (Valorie) (88)
Mrs. Linda Stone (88)
Mrs. Larry Strickland (Montie) (91)
Mrs. Jim Stripling (Debbie)
Mrs. Kyle Tatum (Kathy) (92)
Mrs. Earnest Taylor (Jan) (84)
Mrs. Robert W. Teller (Nancy) (86)
Mrs. Gene Terrell (Joyce) (85)
Mrs. Robert Tumperi (Barbara) (88)
Ms. Lisa Van Houten (93)
Mrs. Phil Vincent (Mary Anna)
Mrs. Donald Walls (Leigh) (92)
Mrs. Jimmy Whitlock (Clare) (88)
Mrs. Shirley Widner (89)
Mrs. Hal Williams (Penny) (90)
Mrs. Gary Wright (Leroyce) (86)
Mrs. Pat Yancey, III (Julie) (90)
Mrs. Bill Yeager (Cindy) (93)

NEWNAN JUNIOR SERVICE LEAGUE
GOLDEN SUSTAINERS
1993-1994

Mrs. Frances Arnall (W)
Mrs. William Arnall (Linda)
Mrs. Sam Banks (Mary Willie) (W)
Mrs. C.M. Barron (Lavinia)
Mrs. Harold Barron (Catherine)
Mrs. Lindsey Barron(Genet)
Mrs. Thomas W. Barron(Margaret)
Mrs. James Beavers, Jr.(Alice)
Mrs. Marion Beavers (Ann)
Mrs. Duke Blackburn(Julia) (W)
Mrs. Brack Blalock(Eleanor) (W)
Mrs. Keith Brady (Katie)
Mrs. Bill Breed (Ann)
Mrs. Herb Bridges (Eleanor)
Ms. Barbara Brown
Mrs. David R. Brown (Rita)
Mrs. R.A. Brown , Jr. (Lynn)
Mrs. Everett Bryant (Mary) (W)
Mrs. Warren Budd (Courtenay)
Mrs. Robert Campbell (Fran)
Mrs. John J. Cenkner (Sandra)
Mrs. Ed Cole (Sarah Gray)(W)
Mrs. Frank Cole, Jr. (Louise)(W)
Mrs. Madison Cole (Martha) (W)
Mrs. Charles Connally (Rosa)
Mrs. Ed Craft (Brenda)
Mrs. Ellis Crook (Pat)
Mrs. Molly Davis
Mrs. Richard Day (Gayle)
Mrs. Ronald Duffey (Lynn)
Mrs. Willis Edwards (Catherine) (W)
Mrs. W.Y. Ellis (Ida) (W)
Mrs. Charles Farmer (Elsie)

Mrs. Hugh Farmer, Jr. (Charlsie)
Mrs. Jett Fisher (Carol) (W)
Mrs. Oliver Gentry (Florine)
Mrs. Herman Glass (Catherine)
Mrs. Cliff Glover (Inez)
Mrs. Howard C.Glover, Jr. (Margaret)
Mrs. J. L. Glover, Sr. (Margaret)
Mrs. John Gray (Alice)
Mrs. John Goodrum (Marsha)
Mrs. Larry Hansen (Karen)
Mrs. James Hardin (Louise)
Mrs. Will Haugen (Evelyn)
Mrs. William Headley (Anita)
Mrs. R.B. Hubbard (Eleanor) (W)
Mrs. Tom Johnson
Mrs. Babe Jenkins
Ms. Julie Jones
Mrs. R.O. Jones (Evelyn) (W)
Mrs. Aaron Keheley (Alberta) (W)
Mrs. Wilkins Kirby, Jr. (Alice)
Mrs. Ed Klein (Winnie Boone) (W)
Mrs. Nathan Knight (Ann)
Mrs. Billy Lee (Susan)
Mrs. Bobby Lee (Pam)
Mrs. Bob Lines (Alice)
Mrs. Wright Lipford (Faye)
Mrs. Howard McCullough (Barbara)
Mrs. Bill McWaters (Linda)
Mrs. V.E. Manget, Jr. (Catherine) (W)
Mrs. Bob Mann (Frances)
Mrs. James Mann (Frances) (W)
Mrs. Taft Mansour (Marguerite) (W)
Mrs. Clarence Moody (Virginia) (W)
Mrs. Parnell Odom (Pat)

NEWNAN JUNIOR SERVICE LEAGUE
GOLDEN SUSTAINERS
1993-1994
(Continued)

Mrs. Terry Overton (Mary)
Mrs. Gene Owen (Judy)
Mrs. James Owens (Elon)
Mrs. Henry Payton (Rosemary)
Mrs. Lavergne Peterson (W)
Mrs. Irwin Pike (Helen) (W)
Mrs. Bill Pinson (Ola)
Mrs. J.H. Powell (Skeez)
Mrs. Roy Power (Judy) (W)
Mrs. Oliver Reason (Annette)
Mrs. Howard Royal (Mary)
Mrs. Robert Royal (Sue)
Mrs. Leigh Sanders (Martha)
Mrs. Walter Sanders (Clara Berry) (W)
Ms. Inez Slaton

Mrs. Charles Smith (Lynn)
Mrs. Michael Smith (Debbie)
Mrs. Maurice Sponcler (Dot)
Mrs. Tommy Strother (Frances)
Mrs. John Stuckey (Sandy)
Mrs. Steve Threlkeld (Genny)
Mrs. Don Tomlinson (Jane)
Mrs. Dan Umbach (Marie)
Mrs. Jean Wagner
Mrs. Jimmy Weddington (Mary)
Mrs. John White (Martha)
Mrs. Bruce Williams (Sandra)
Mrs. Carl E. Williams (Eddy)
Mrs. Minerva Woodroof
Mrs. Pat Yacey, Jr. (Jeanne)

(W) Widow

A Taste of Georgia, *Another Serving*
Newnan Junior Service League, Inc.
P.O. Box 1433
Newnan, Georgia 30264

Please send_____copies of **A Taste of Georgia,** *Another Serving* at
$14.95 per book plus $2.50 for postage and handling for each book. Georgia
residents please add $.90 sales tax per book.

Name _____

Address _____

City_____State_____Zip_____

Make checks payable to **A Taste of Georgia,** *Another Serving.* All previous coupons void.

A Taste of Georgia, *Another Serving*
Newnan Junior Service League, Inc.
P.O. Box 1433
Newnan, Georgia 30264

Please send_____copies of **A Taste of Georgia,** *Another Serving* at
$14.95 per book plus $2.50 for postage and handling for each book. Georgia
residents please add $.90 sales tax per book.

Name _____

Address _____

City_____State_____Zip_____

Make checks payable to **A Taste of Georgia,** *Another Serving.* All previous coupons void.

A Taste of Georgia, *Another Serving*
Newnan Junior Service League, Inc.
P.O. Box 1433
Newnan, Georgia 30264

Please send_____copies of **A Taste of Georgia,** *Another Serving* at
$14.95 per book plus $2.50 for postage and handling for each book. Georgia
residents please add $.90 sales tax per book.

Name _____

Address _____

City_____State_____Zip_____

Make checks payable to **A Taste of Georgia,** *Another Serving.* All previous coupons void.